Rise and Progress of a Village

LINDA RENÉ-MARTIN

ISBN 0 9533573 0 9
Designed and published by the Author Linda René-Martin
Coast Cottage, Sandgate, Kent CT20 3DA
Produced by Chameleon Design Consultants, Swingfield, Kent CT15 7HF
Printed by A.R. Adams & Sons (Printers) Ltd, Dover, Kent CT16 1EW

'NEW INN' Sandgate c.1811. Recruiting officer presses the King's shilling on the tipsy yokels. Watercolour, Lt.Col. William Henry Ford. William Drummond ©

For

my dear Friends and

Defenders of Sandgate

GEOFFREY* AND ANN EDMUNDS

*Chairman 1988-97 and President

The Sandgate Society

Folkestone Hundred and, to west of Horn St., Hearne Hundred. From Topographical Map of the County of Kent, published by Jonathan Andrews, Andrew Drury and William Herbert, 1769. By kind permission H. Margary, Lympne Castle.

CONTENTS:

Introduction

SANDGATE is still as Cobbett noted in 1823 on his Rural Ride through Kent – 'a beautiful little place upon the beach itself'. Set on a narrow stretch of land, to the North it is confined by steep richly-wooded slopes rising, at times, 250 ft to army ground at Shorncliffe and, to the South, by the English Channel. To the East, the A259 from Folkestone winds sharply down to Sandgate High Street, passing through the age-old village, then skirts the scenic shoreline west to Hythe.

The village endures the forces of nature. The northern slopes, the source of many springs, are geologically unstable and major landslips are recorded in 1827 and 1893*. It has suffered coast erosion and has withstood the onslaughts of the boisterous English Channel. But setbacks fade and seaside joys prevail when Sandgate views the silvery sweep of bay to Dungeness and hears the lazy lapping on the shore.

Historically, Sandgate was once a little bastion against invasion. Today, six gaunt Martello Towers on the heights, a peaceful Castle on the pebble shore, the lure of the French cliffs clear in the evening light, the Channel Tunnel not far off, remind us that those days of strife are over.

On the administrative side, in 1934 Sandgate is merged reluctantly with Folkestone Borough Council, absorbed in Shepway District Council in 1974. Despite modern expansion, Sandgate proudly guards its identity and its sense of history. Through the efforts of The Sandgate Society, two large Conservation Areas (designated 1972) now help to protect a fascinating mix of architectural styles. Examples of Kent weatherboarded cottages, balconied stucco terraces, villas built of ragstone or solid brick with hanging tiles, reflect late Georgian, Victorian and Edwardian eras and into the present. The Castle (1539), the Parish Church of St Paul (1850), the former National School (1866) at the foot of Sandgate Hill, the former Volunteer Fire Station (1884) and Spade House (1901) home of H.G. Wells, attract the eye. Notable architects and skilled craftsmen have left their mark.

Economically, Sandgate has always adapted to changing times and needs. Its rise and progress clearly stem from the late 18th century days of shipbuilding for George III's Navy. With the Napoleonic menace, the growing presence of the Military at Shorncliffe Camp (est.1794), brings life and trade to the village; lodgings, inns and taverns are in demand. When peace returns, it flowers as a select and serene little watering place, long before Folkestone or Hythe. The revival of the Camp in the days of Imperial rule spurs the economy. Then post World War II, Sandgate develops as the South-east centre of the Antiques Trade. In 1998, a new era opens up with the completion of the £25 million ultra-modern base in Enbrook Park for SAGA Group's activities.

Through all its vicissitudes, Sandgate survives as a caring, close-knit community. In many walks of life, it embraces well-known, well-loved characters – religious, military, literary, commercial – and a colourful social history unfolds.

*A Survey of the Coastal Landslides of Kent – Professor J.N.Hutchinson for Min.of Technology Building Research Station (EN/35/65). Recent public works (1992-96) have reduced the risk

Sandgate Castle and coastline to Hythe, 1765. After a drawing by H. Foucquet 1733. Kent County Records.
DIDO, 28-gun frigate built 1784 by Stewart & Hall, attacks French warships MINERVE and ARTEMISE off Minorca, 24 June 1795. National Maritime Museum Greenwich ©

War and Peace

Lt.Gen. Sir John Moore. Statue on Sandgate Esplanade

Romans, Saxons, Danes, Normans – all have landed on our Kentish shore and defence of the realm becomes paramount.

1256 SANDYGEAT, as first recorded, denotes a gate or cleft in the sandstone hills through which the Enbrook flows to meet the sea. No more than a dot on the landscape Sandgate, strategically, has to be on watch. According to 13th C. Rolls, the Manor of Stowting is duty-bound to keep a constable and six men 'to guard the passage of the sea' at Sandgate.

Sangatte in the Calais region, according to French sources (1924) derives from 'Sandgate' as the area was known under English rule 1347-1558, also shown as Sandegate or Sangat in State papers. But prior to the 15th C. it was known as Seclives or Sclives. Its early church of St. Martin appears in Archbishop Morton's register (March 1497) at 'Sandgate alias Slymys' alternately 'Slymes comté Guines'. It overlooked an inlet or anchorage on a vast sandy shore. The Saxon church of St. Martin, Parish of Cheriton (burial place of Sandgate folk) is just across the Channel.

1539 During the Reformation, when relations with France and Spain are strained to the limit, Henry VIII orders the building of Sandgate Castle along with those at Walmer, Deal, Sandown, and Camber to defend *agaynste the intolerable yoke of Popish tyranie.* Fortifications expert, Stephanus de Hashenperg *(sic)* is in charge and ledgers in the British Library show its completion within 19 months at a final cost of £5,587.5s.10 $^{1}/_{8}$d, itemised to the last nail and farthing. The Enbrook stream supplies water. On 3 September 1539 Thomas Cockes (Comptroller of the Castle) reports to Cromwell (Lord Privy Seal): *The Castle at Sandgate within your Lordship of Folkestone, is well brought forward. Three towers ready to be covered; which Stephen the Almain*... would have covered with canvas, pitch and tar. Thinks lead would be better, of which there is enough to cover whole Castle.* Henry VIII pays two visits, March 1541 and May 1542. (*i.e. Allemand or German. Mary of Hungary refers to Stephen van Hassenpergk, a gentleman of Moravia).

1573 Fifteen years before the defeat of the Spanish Armada, Queen Elizabeth I dines and rests at the the Castle on her way from Westenhanger to Dover. Thereafter, it is held by a Constable and a few soldiers while the sea takes its toll.

1652 In August, during the 1st Dutch wars, the main Dutch fleet under Cornelius de With sails down Channel behind de Ruyter, driving half a dozen merchantmen ashore between Folkestone and Hythe and passes, it is said, so close as to be fired upon from Sandgate Castle.

COMMAND OF THE SEAS: The latter part of the 18th C. sees one of the most turbulent eras in English naval history when hostilities with France, Spain, Holland and the North American colonies are at a peak. England's prosperity is linked with her far-flung colonies and naval supremacy is vital. Sandgate with an ample foreshore plays a part in this. Shipbuilding starts up and a village evolves.

1773 Coinciding with the year of the 'Boston Tea Party', Fabian Clayton Wilson is the first to set up shipyards, on beachy ground leased from the 2nd Earl of Radnor. Wilson prospers and builds himself a spacious residence (possibly the site of The Hermitage), and some thirty tenements for his men. Two centuries later, several cottages survive at the foot of Sandgate Hill.

1775-87 Other shipwrights follow, notably Phineas Jacob and Stewart & Hall. Seven 28-gun frigates, four 16-gun sloops and two fire ships are built for H.M. Navy. The 28-gun *ROSE,* a beautifully mounted ship with carved work is launched, fully-manned, from the steeply shelving beach (June 1783).

1814-73 After Waterloo, Thomas Lowes, Sherlock, Ayres and Graves continue the trade – brigs, yawls, luggers and fishing craft – but on a lesser scale. Lowes of Knoll House, boatbuilder to the King of the Belgians (post 1830), becomes implicated in a notorious smuggling affray and, defended by Lord Brougham, is acquitted. Richard Graves, Sandgate's last boatbuilder, gives up trade in 1873.

1794 **MILITARY CONCERNS:** Shorncliffe Camp is established on the heights overlooking Sandgate. The War Dept. purchases 229 acres of open land, and more in 1796 and 1806. Temporary wooden barracks are replaced in 1804 with more solid structures in stone, to house cavalry and artillery. In the lee of the Camp, Sandgate grows and prospers.

1803-5 The Castle is on watch again. Peace with France, under the Treaty of Amiens, has been brief and 25 miles across the Channel, Napoleon and his Grande Armée are poised to conquer England. While the English fleet blockades the French ports, Pitt orders plans for the defence of the Kent and Sussex coast. At Shorncliffe Camp Sir John Moore, pioneer of light infantry training, commands the coast from Deal to Dungeness. He writes: *I cannot persuade myself that Bonaparte will be mad enough to attempt it . . . the invasion would, I am confident, end in our glory and in his disgrace.*

Sandgate's westerly defences are extended (Battery Point) and the Royal Military Canal, conceived by the great civil engineer John Rennie, begins its slow construction under Lt.Col. John Brown, 25 miles across Romney Marsh to Rye and beyond. Some years earlier, Capt.William Henry Ford (c.1770-1829) of the Corps of Royal Engineers, advocates *Towers as Sea Fortresses,* on the Corsican model, in a memorandum to Brig.General Twiss. Seventy four Martello Towers are now hurriedly erected, of 27 in Kent Nos 4 to 9 above Sandgate itself. The crumbling Castle is transformed into a giant Martello armed with cannon. Cobbett inveighs in Republican spirit (1823): *Martello Towers...OH, Lord ! to think that I should be destined to behold these monuments to the wisdom of Pitt and Dundas and Perceval! Good God! Here they are, piles of bricks in circular form, about 40 feet high, and about 150 feet circumference at the top...Cannons are to be fired from the top of these things, in order to defend the country against French Jacobins!*

1809 Lt.Gen.Sir John Moore* during the Peninsular Wars dies (16 January) at the strategic victory at Corunna. *The honest loved him; the dishonest feared him...Such a combination of acknowledged fame, of devotion from all who served under him...sentiments of honour as exalted as his practice.* One hundred years later, a fine bronze bust on a granite plinth is placed on Sandgate Esplanade, close to his temporary quarters.

1809-12 Lt.Col.W.H.Ford (later Lt. Governor of the Royal Military Academy Woolwich) is posted to Dover Command HQ under General Sir David Dundas and Brig.General Twiss. His plans for coastal defences include works to secure the left flank of the Royal Military Canal with a Redoubt near the sluice gate at Seabrook; also the Battery walls and embrasures on Sandgate's seafront, and the New Road (Military Hill) leading to the Royal Artillery Establishment at Shorncliffe. Ford is also a 'Sunday painter' with a keen eye for the local scene.

1815 Napoleon abdicates after the Allies – under Wellington and Blücher – triumph at Waterloo. Late in June, the Kent coast resounds to a salvo of guns to welcome the crowned heads of Europe as they sail into Dover on route to the Victory Celebrations in London. According to John Gough's mother, many a pane is shattered by the force of the 24-pounder atop Sandgate Castle.

1849 Since the end of the Napoleonic Wars, much of Shorncliffe Camp has reverted to grazing land but, as Thomas Rammell reports, 150 acres are still used by the Board of Ordnance. These constitute *one of the finest exercise grounds in the Kingdom, the dry and healthy conditions being especially beneficial to troops newly returned from foreign service.*

1855 Queen Victoria and Prince Albert pass through Sandgate on their way to Shorncliffe Camp to inspect the British German Legion, destined for the Crimea wars. In fact, the Armistice of 1856 sees many dispersed, disbanded or offered a chance to go to the Cape as colonists. Their place is filled by 5000 British troops back from heroic service in the Crimea under Sir Colin Campbell.

1860 Europe is in ferment; Lord Palmerston mis-trusts the French and obtains a £9 million vote to bolster dockyards and national defences. Sandgate Castle is rearmed but, in the end, only the Artillery Volunteers use the guns for drill and practice fire.

1861-2 Palmerston pays two visits to Shorncliffe Camp. On the second occasion he presides at the presentation of a tribute from the County of Ross and Cromarty to the Seaforth Highlanders for distinguished action at the relief of Lucknow and Cawnpore (Indian Mutiny 1857-59).

1881-93 The Royal Standard is hoisted for the last time. The War Office sells the Castle (destined for a Railway Station !) for £20,000 to the South Eastern Railway Co. whose scheme to run a seafront line through Sandgate to Folkestone Harbour is vehemently opposed. For one, General Hankey on Radnor Cliff would resent a steam-train beneath his kitchen window. In 1893 the Castle first opens to the public (22 August) under the auspices of the Sandgate Improvement and Publicity Assn. accompanied by the band of the 1st Cinque Ports Artillery Volunteers.

*b.1761 KB Nov 1804, Lt.Gen. Nov 1805

1890 The Barracks Act authorizes the expenditure of £4 million out of the Consolidated Fund and out of moneys to be provided by Parliament, for the building and enlarging of camps and barracks in the United Kingdom and in certain colonies. This reinforces the peace-keeping, trading role of the Empire. Shorncliffe is allocated £170,000, wooden huts are replaced by brick quarters, and sanitary arrangements improved. For the next 50 years, the Camp is the mainstay of Sandgate in terms of trade and jobs. (*Roy Brook MA Thesis, Bangor Univ. 1962*). The village has a military tailor and bootmaker till the 1940's.

1893 For boys who love to play 'soldiers' nothing fires the spirit like a visit to the Camp. *The Holiday Annual* (10 June) recounts a family ramble, the short climb from Sandgate, the lovely view, the air exhilirating: *But the Camp – oh! the Camp. There was a fear that I should have three young 'soldiers' to bring home. Many an hour we spent watching redcoats, bluecoats, whitecoats and anything that held a gun or a sword and to see the cavalry galloping to the tune of 'Bonnie Dundee' was the height of happiness. Many a rest we had in the gymnasium watching the drill or laughing at the clumsy attempts of some new recruit to imitate his betters.*

Martello garrison c.1811, bedding and 'messing'. Watercolour W.H. Ford. William Drummond ©

1900 In April, amid fanfare and flags, vast crowds turn out to welcome the Ladysmith Heroes to The Beach Rocks Convalescent Home, after a 6-month siege and a 6000 mile journey. By 1908 The Beach Rocks is known as the Alfred Bevan Memorial Convalescent Home where the splendid, somewhat formidable Sister Mumford takes charge of 200 persons, in particular the wounded in World War I.

1909 The Helena Hospital for the families of the military is completed at a cost of £10,000. It is perched above Battery Point and replaces the 'Black Hut', (an early Coastguard Watch) which, barely holding 15 patients is demolished in 1906.

1914 World War I breaks out and by 1915, 40,000 Canadians are in training at Shorncliffe Camp. The Castle is used as an air-raid shelter and by the Royal Field Artillery.

1916 A posthumous VC is awarded to Lance Corporal William Cotter, East Kent Regt. (the 'Buffs') of 2 Barton Cottages. His memorial is in the Chichester Hall.

1918 In terms of life and limb, a devastating War has ended. Sandgate resumes the daily round. As always, it hears the haunting sounds of Reveille and Last Post drifting down from the Camp – a reminder of a military training ground, of wars themselves and their tragic aftermath.

1919 The British Red Cross Society acquires Enbrook House and grounds as a seaside branch of the Star and Garter Hospital in Richmond and the Medical Staff believe it will be of the greatest boon to the seriously disabled. The Red Cross also conveys land at the foot of Military Rd to the Urban District Council for Sandgate's Memorial to the Dead. This notes that a bomb exploded nearby, 15 May 1917.

1920 In August, the disabled are moved from Richmond to temporary quarters in Enbrook House, pending the rebuilding. After their return to Richmond in 1924, Enbrook House is entirely redesigned by Sir Edwin Cooper FRIBA, *(below)* but incorporating Teulon's imposing east wall, oriel window and carriage entrance.

1928 Sandgate's air is deemed especially beneficial and the Star and Garter maintains Enbrook as a holiday home for around 70 disabled ex-Servicemen. Those who can, engage in handicrafts, keep chickens and grow most of their own vegetables. In their wheelchairs, they are a touching and familiar sight and Sandgate shows concern.

1939-40 World War II and invasion fears are rife. For safety, the disabled are sent to Richmond and Enbrook House is requisitioned by the Army and later the National Fire Service.

Demolished Jan 1996
Collection Chris Phillips

1946 The Sandgate Star and Garter branch is leased to the Home Office. It is opened by Sir Frank Soskice in July 1947 as No. 6 District Police Training Centre. In 1977 Inter-City Tours Ltd (SAGA Holidays) acquire the 27-acre property for around £200,000.

World War II **FRONT-LINE VILLAGE:** France surrenders in June 1940. England stands alone and the Battle of Britain rages overhead. Sandgate, 8-10 miles west of Hellfire Corner, and just east of a possible German landing (Operation Sealion), becomes a Defence Area. Security is tight and only those with essential business may remain. Hurriedly, defences are set up; enormous coils of barbed wire; mines and anti-tank traps in the beach; pill-boxes camouflaged as bathing huts or kiosks and 'dummies' (for want of guns) along the shoreline. The Castle is mounted with anti-aircraft guns and serves as an Air-raid shelter and Home Guard post. Shorncliffe AA batteries are on the alert. Unlike the massive bombing and shelling of Folkestone and Dover, the village mainly suffers parachute-mine and offshore blast. In March 1942, two houses in Chichester Road are severely damaged, and one a 'write-off'. In January 1943, an enemy bomb lands in the Star and Garter grounds, causing damage to St. Paul's, the empty Sandgate Primary School and around 100 homes nearby. Three other bombs drop harmlessly offshore. In 1944, the Doodle-bugs (VI's) are droning over; one skims the 'Gents' at the Seapoint Café on the Esplanade, nearly catching a lad with his pants down. Other missiles are brought down near the shore. Inevitably houses and shops are badly shaken, and windows boarded up.

1945 The Boulogne guns are silent. VE Day celebrations (8 May), marking the end of World War II in Europe, include a children's party in Wilberforce Road with games, races, music and dancing, and ending with cheers for the organisers.

1949-50 The semi-derelict Castle and land attached (sold in 1927) is seriously damaged by the sea and the South bastion totally destroyed. Much of the stone is used to repair the main seawall. In 1954 the Black family acquire Castle Close and the Castle which comes with it.

1974 The Civic Amenities Act 1967 (following the Historic Buildings and Ancient Monuments Act 1953) requires the protection and improvement of buildings of architectural or historic interest and a Local Authority shall make some provision for this, under its supervision. Sandgate Castle is a Grade I Listed and Scheduled Ancient Monument. With Planning Consent, the Drs Peter and Barbara MacGregor (née Black) make Herculean efforts to restore the the fabric, privately, and mainly at their own expense.

1987 The restored Castle, as notified to Shepway Council by letter 26 March, is open to public view; also for banquets, cultural and social events. Still with Tudor traces, it is a history book in stone.

1998 The restoration and upkeep of the Castle has placed an over-whelming burden on the owners. This ancient stronghold, the very core of Sandgate history, has been repossessed by Lloyds Bank and now awaits a modern 'knight in shining armour' to be its guardian.

1999 Two thousand Ghurkas are expected to take up married quarters. According to National Defence policy, Shorncliffe Garrison is maintained but on a lesser scale. The Military Cemetery dates from the mid 1850's. Annually on Canada Day, tribute is paid to the 296 Canadians buried there.

Administration and Public Health

SANDGATE, as a social entity, has no roots until the shipwrights set up yards on beachy 'wasteland' and are in need of shelter, food and drink. Unlike Hythe and Folkestone it enjoys no ancient charters and privileges, but falls within an outworn system centred on the parish vestry. Divided by the Enbrook stream, Sandgate is a hybrid place within two parishes: 310 acres in Cheriton, 220 acres in Folkestone, while to the east on rising ground it takes in some 30 acres of the Township of Folkestone.

1832 The creation of the Parliamentary District of Hythe and Folkestone results from the momentous Reform Act and includes Sandgate.

1834 Under the Poor Law Amendment Act, fifteen parishes are grouped in the Elham Poor Law Union. Paupers and vagrants are lodged in the dreaded workhouse at Etchinghill, under the eye of a Board of Guardians (abolished 1929). Typhoid, cholera and other diseases are rife in England, especially in the slums. In Sandgate, there is no distinct governing body armed with legal powers to enforce proper sanitary regulations and competent to undertake such works. As a little resort rising in repute, Sandgate must pave its streets and fend for itself, by voluntary contribution.

1846 The Rev. Rawdon Greene plans the Undercliffe Estate and employs Messrs Grissell and Peto (eminent civil engineers) to underdrain the hillside and provide spring water to 56 houses.

1848 The first Public Health Act results from the cholera menace and the controlling efforts of Edwin Chadwick, one of the Poor Law Commissioners – notably his *Report of the Sanitary Conditions of the Labouring Population* in 1842 and the Royal Commission's Report, 1844, into the *Sanitary State of Large Towns and Populous Districts.* A whole new era opens up when Sandgate (among 62 towns without councils) is enabled to carry out town improvement.

1849 A Superintending Inspector, Thomas Webster Rammell, assesses *the present destitute sanitary condition* of the town, (including 23 dunghills, 14 piggeries and four offensive slaughter houses) and makes recommendations. He reports to the General Board of Health, Whitehall: *I have the satisfaction to state that I noticed in the inhabitants generally, and especially in the more influential of them, a strong disposition to forward the objects of the inquiry, and that every possible facility for obtaining information was readily accorded to me.* His Second Report (1850) defines, with local agreement and that of Lord Radnor, the boundaries of the proposed Local Board of Health, enclosing much of Radnor Cliff.

1850 The first Sandgate Local Board of Health comes into being with nine elected members, and the Rev. S.J. Gambier (Perpetual Curate) as Chairman. Like Boards elsewhere, it has powers to borrow from Central Government, to levy a local rate and draw up bye-laws. All habitations are to be provided with running water, WC's and drainage with money borrowed against the rate. Progress covers an improved supply of water, public gas lighting, the appointment of a scavenger, and an Inspector of Nuisances. Sandgate, with a population of around 1400 is chosen as a model of what can be done in a village.

1852 Members of the General Board of Health (Whitehall) are impressed: *The same public spirit which [has] achieved these blessings may be relied upon to complete the very little which is yet to be done in the way of street paving and surface drainage* (11 August).

1853 George Moseley a local surgeon, in his book *Sandgate as a Residence for Invalids,* sets out to extol its virtues, its gentle climate, freedom from fog and its facilities for the cure of every ailment from dyspepsia to liver disorders and tuberculosis.

1854 A serious outbreak of cholera alarms the village, of 94 reported cases 46 prove fatal. Thomas E. Blackwell CE reports (Feb.1855) to Whitehall on the defective jointing of drains, and analyses the state of wells and of water supply which derives from three sources. (Cherry Garden Reservoir, hillside at Shorncliffe and high ground near Castle Hole).

1858 The Local Board of Health consults Mr. Homersham CE who advises the purchase of two springs – The Upper and Lower Honeywood Springs above Seabrook, known for their exceptional purity (closed 1964).

1859 Two Acts (1858) – The Jewish Relief Act and the Oaths Act – remove disabilities and allow the House of Commons and the House of Lords each to administer its own form of oath. Baron Mayer de Rothschild takes his seat as Liberal MP for Hythe and Folkestone District (1859-74) and in 1899 Sir Edward Sassoon (who leases Shorncliffe Lodge in Sandgate) sits as Liberal Unionist till 1912. Balfour, Lloyd George and Winston Churchill are among the guests. His equally able son, Sir Philip, follows as MP (1912-39) residing later at 'Port Lympne' but often seen at Sandgate events.

c.1859 A Volunteer Fire Brigade now exists but lacks quarters and adequate equipment. The Local Board has no statutory powers to fund it and it is supported entirely by public subscription. In 1884, through the generosity of the Misses Reilly of Encombe and local people, the Brigade takes up splendid quarters in the High St. and is renowned for its efficiency. *Vive les sapeurs-pompiers d' Angleterre* becomes the toast in France.

1882 Sandgate tidies up. Clerk to the Local Board reports (f.1515): *You will also be glad to hear that the last of the pigs have been removed from Mill Lane (Gough Road) and…it has now become quite a respectable thoroughfare.*

1887-9 Folkestone Municipal Borough makes a first attempt to annex the whole of the Local Government District of Sandgate, mainly for drainage and rating purposes. It is a complex and vexing issue and Sandgate makes counter-proposals.

1890' s This decade is beset with problems, struggles and disasters. F.M. Hueffer (Ford Madox Ford) writes: *I do not remember ever to have passed through the place without seeing works of some sort in progress. In the winter the sea is engaged in making gaps; throughout the rest of the year the local authorities in repairing them.* In 1889 and again in 1896, the Esplanade and horse-drawn tramway ('The Toastrack') between Hythe and Folkestone, is badly undermined. The Sandgate Landslip of 1893 is a major crisis.

1894 The Local Board of Health becomes an Urban District Council with powers under the new Local Government Act. It uses the Public Reading Room as a Council Chamber and Lt. Col. R.J. Fynmore becomes first Chairman, already serving 12 times as Chairman of the Local Board.

1895/6 The 'Boundary Question' hots-up again. The Folkestone Boundaries Extension Bill comes before a House of Lords Committee. Among others, the Rev. Russell Wakefield, a former Chairman of the Local Board, states that Sandgate has nothing to gain by amalgamation. Finally, the Lords decide that it is not expedient to proceed with the Bill. Sandgate maintains its autonomy. Folkestone, however, persists. In 1896 it attempts to obtain a Provisional Order and Sandgate is obliged to petition against its confirmation and is confident of success. (UDC Minutes 5 Oct.)

1898 Sandgate UDC scores another triumph and makes legal history. Following a 7-year battle, the House of Lords decides that the County Council is liable for the upkeep of the sea defences forming part of the main road system (A259). Sandgate avoids a crippling bill and the decision sets a precedent for every seaside town.

1900 The turn of the century brings forward-looking changes. Streets are renamed, such as Chapel Street to Wilberforce Road; Mill Lane to Gough Road; Broadway to the High Street. Houses are renumbered from the 'Fleur de Lis' to the Coastguard Station. A new Post Office is completed and by 1903, electric lighting is turned on.

1904 Jane Hester Reilly of Encombe dies, but the land she provided for the Volunteer Fire Station and Public Reading Room has never been 'deeded'. Before her death, her nieces obtain power of attorney and convey the land and premises to the Sandgate Urban District Council for the sum of £650.

1905 An upsurge of unregulated nursing homes causes concern. The Sandgate UDC (Sanitary powers) Act provides for 'the licensing and control of hospitals for diseases and other provisions for the health of the district, and for other purposes.' This applies to workers in dairies, laundries, businesses, and to the control of infections in general.

1934 Sandgate Urban District Council (bounded by Coolinge Lane) is finally absorbed by Folkestone Borough Council (Local Government Act 1933, later repealed). Local Government becomes party political. The Sandgate Ward which includes Shorncliffe and a large part of west Folkestone, is represented by three councillors. The Chairman's splendid chain of office is now worn by the Deputy Mayor of Folkestone. Sandgate disappears from the road signs. From now on, it struggles to maintain its identity.

Chairmen, Local Board of Health. Left: *Lt.Col. R.J. Fynmore.* Right: *the Rev. S.J. Gambier*

John B. Gough, reformed alcoholic and temperance orator, b. Sandgate 1817

John 4th Earl of Darnley of Cobham Hall and Enbrook. Engraving c.1816

1962 Sandgate lacks a Parish Council to defend and promote its interests. The Sandgate Society is founded (Mrs Estelle Greenwall JP, Chairman) to campaign against destruction and neglect, to protect the village character, trees and footpaths, and improve amenities where possible.

1974 May 1st, under the Reorganisation of Local Government Act 1972, Folkestone ceases to be a Borough and comes under the umbrella of Shepway District Council. The Folkestone/Sandgate Ward is redefined.

1988 Sandgate's NHS Surgery, in the Crescent, closes down when Drs. Lendon and Ewer retire. The Kent Family Practitioners Committee considers that the panel of around 1000 patients is 'below the national average' and the S.E. Thames Regional Health Authority decides not to appoint a successor. Patients are obliged to go to Hythe or Folkestone. Chaplin' s the Chemist and Pharmacy, successor to Jenner's, loses custom and closes after 150 years of unbroken service to the community.

1998 For several years, exceptionally heavy rainfall and flash floods have caused the Pent and Enbrook streams to wreak havoc in Folkestone and Sandgate. Sandgate is given its own flood warden to deal with emergencies. Southern Water Authority decides to renew part of the ancient drainage system in Sandgate and outfall to the sea. Larger pipes will now convey an increased volume of storm water, and the building of a new storm tank will help to alleviate flooding. This is part of an overall £120 million scheme to improve bathing water quality and reduce the risk of flooding in the Folkestone/Dover area. A great plus for Sandgate.

Religion, Education and Morality

SANDGATE an isolated village falls, since early times, within two parishes, Cheriton and Folkestone, and virtually fends for itself. When William Wilberforce MP arrives in July 1812, the nearest place of worship and of burial is still the Saxon church of St. Martin's up Horn Street, half an hour by pony. Against the radical and irreligious forces of the day, Wilberforce, the Slave Trade Abolitionist and leader of the Evangelical movement, finds Sandgate sadly godless and vulnerable.

On the first of four long summer visits with his family in 1812-13-14 and 1825, Wilberforce writes to his brother-in-law, the Evangelical James Stephen: *It is grievous to see this place, hot and cold baths, library, billiard tables, ponies, donkeys, everything but a church, or chapel or anything of the kind though it is a sort of preserve of the Archbishop's. There is not even a Sunday School...we are trying to get something of the kind set on foot.*

1814 Wilberforce prevails on the War Department to lease out premises near the Castle where village children are taught at 1d a week on Dr. Bell's system. In November, Marianne Francis, a niece of Fanny Burney and companion to his children, writes to a friend: *The adult school was established just before we left Sandgate, teaching and a room provided, and all left in good train. Dear Mr W went himself, read them instances from Pole's History of Adult Schools, a book you ought to see – made them a little speech saying how much he respected their good sense for coming, and fairly seated himself by their side, in good earnest, and began hearing them say their letters...highly useful and encouraging in its effects upon the institution.*

1816 The Methodists pioneer Sandgate's first place of worship in Chapel Street. (later renamed Wilberforce Road). The Established Church is under pressure to follow.

1822 At his sole cost, John 4th Earl of Darnley provides a Chapel of Ease on the edge of his Enbrook estate, designed by George Stanley Repton (1786-1858) 4th son of Humphry Repton, to seat 250 people. It is enlarged several times, before damage by fire in 1848.

1843 The extension of the South Eastern Railway to Folkestone, and later a Sandgate branch near Battery Point (1874-1931), brings an influx of visitors, new residents, and prosperity in general. Within two decades (1831-51) Sandgate's summer population almost doubles to around 1400 souls. For the gentry, gracious villas appear along Radnor Cliff and Undercliffe; genteel teaching academies are started, but basic education for the poor lacks funds and space.

1845 Lord Melbourne's Government, in 1839, has increased capital grants towards school buildings, and the School Sites Act of 1841 enables the Lord of the Manor to deed waste or common land in order to educate poor persons in religious and useful knowledge. As a result Sandgate's first National School, initially for 44 boys, 40 girls and 70 infants, is built by public grant and private subscription, near the Castle on land deeded by Lord Radnor. John Gough (1817-86) world famous Temperance Orator, once a poor Sandgate boy and migrant to America, beholds in 1855 the changes since his childhood: *Ah! I see now – the village green where fairs were held, is gone, and there is a large National School...not so picturesque but more practical, [facing the humble dwelling where he was born].*

Top: *Chapel of Ease 1822. Gift of the 4th Earl of Darnley, architect George Stanley Repton. No 4 Martello far left. Published by the Misses Purday, Sandgate.* Below: *Church of St Paul (S.S. Teulon 1850) and to right, Church of England Primary School (P.C. Hardwick 1866).* Aerofilms 1920 ©

1849 Religion, in all its sects and forms, is seen as a spiritual need and a morally binding force in a fast expanding village, and a larger church is necessary. At the expense of the Hon. Sir John Duncan Bligh KCB (surviving brother of the 5th Earl of Darnley) and other benefactors, the Church of St Paul replaces Repton's Chapel. Provided with a gallery, it can seat 890 people.

S.S. Teulon (1812-73) rising young architect and early proponent of the Gothic revival designs it, also Enbrook House (1852) for the philanthropic Darnley family. A stone tablet set in the East wall reads: *With thy blessing let the house of thy servant be blessed for ever (2 Samuel vii, 29).* Hand in hand, a permanent parsonage is attached to the Living. It is the work of Sydney Smirke (1798-1877) who also draws up a potential Folkestone Town Plan for Lord Radnor. The Rev. S.J. Gambier, notable as first elected Chairman of the Sandgate Local Board of Health (1850) moves in.

1854 By Order in Council, Sandgate is formed into an Ecclesiastical Parish incorporating parts of the civil parishes of Cheriton and Folkestone. The Trustees of the Darnley/Bligh estate retain the benefice till 1888.

1872 On the death of Sir John Duncan Bligh, the right of presentation to the Living falls to the Vicar of Folkestone and at his death reverts to the Archbishop of Canterbury. In 1883 a Vestry is built and, among other benefactions, the Misses Reilly donate a pulpit in 1891 and, in 1892, Mrs Tiffany of New York bestows plush hangings in the Sanctuary.

Later, other places of worship include the Wesleyan Military and Civilian Church (1900 demolished 1974) in the angle of Gough Road and the Congregational Chapel (1863) in the High Street badly shaken in World War II. In 1966 it is converted to the Little Theatre by the FHODS (Folkestone, Hythe Operatic and Dramatic Society).

* * *

PHILANTHROPY: Sandgate mirrors the virtues and vices of the Victorian age in which literacy, morality, sobriety and thrift are to be encouraged. As the 19th century moves on, the nation sees a notable rise in charitable bodies and private benefactions for the care of body and soul. Sandgate, open to rough influences, is no exception. With the support of the local nobility, gentry and townsfolk, institutions are set up for the betterment of village life in general. These include Jenner's Sick Dispensary (1844) for free medical advice and care of the needy; a House of Refuge for young women in need of care and protection; a non-denominational Soldier's Institute opened by Lucy and Octavia Papillon in Chapel Street. (est.1858, moved to Woodforde House 1896); The Gough Coffee Tavern and Soldiers' Home in the High Street (1879) and, in connection with the London Thrift Society, a Penny Bank for schoolchildren and others, run by Richard Fynmore, (later first Manager of the local Lloyds Bank, 1903). In 1875 James Morris Esq., (one of three serving Governors of the Bank of England, 1847,48) endows a sizable dwelling for the deserving poor on Broadway (i.e. The High Street). Lt.Col.William Wheatley, in 1877, provides a drinking fountain and a horse and cattle trough at the start of Sandgate Hill. The London Samaritan Society sets up the Beach Rocks Convalescent Home (1883, enlarged 1892) for crippled children from the London slums. Doctors and Vicars also play their part.

1855 Prince Albert, in 1854, advocates public reading institutions for the intellectual and moral improvement of the people. Sandgate follows with a Working Men's Library and Reading Institution supported by the inhabitants, later known as the Sandgate Literary Institute. Under its auspices, Sunday 'Penny Readings' interspersed with vocal and instrumental music are held in Tom Valyer's Assembly Rooms. In July, that same year, a Committee from the London Temperance League arrives in force and John Gough addresses the cheering children in the National School, with George Cruikshank (satirist and teetotaller) presiding.

1866 A new, more spacious National School, designed in neo-Gothic style by P.C. Hardwick (1792-1870) is erected at the foot of Sandgate Hill, on land deeded by Lord Radnor. It can hold 350 boys and girls, and has a playground and houses for Headmaster and Headmistress attached. James Morris Esq. of Encombe is the sole benefactor ((£6000) and for beauty the School is said to have no rival in the District.

The 1845 National School in Castle Road then becomes a Drill Hall for the Artillery Volunteers. Later used by T/S INVICTA (Folkestone & Hythe Sea Cadets) and Folkestone Detachment ZULU Company, Marine Cadets.

1875 Mr. Pledge, a pious loving man, opens a Mission in the Devonshire Rooms (also the meeting place of the Local Board of Health) to bring mariners and the aged poor who stay away from church and chapel, under religious instruction and influence.

1879 John Gough returns to his native village to lay the foundation stone of The John B. Gough Soldiers Home & Institute on a corner of the High Street. Raised by public subscription, it also has a Coffee Tavern with all profits to the Temperance Movement. (Part of it becomes the Masonic Hall).

1884 The Literary Institute moves to the beautifully panelled Reading Room above the Volunteer Fire Station, built through the generosity of the Reilly sisters of Encombe and public subscription. In February 1888, John Ruskin is staying on Devonshire Terrace and misses Kate Greenaway and teas in Hampstead: *I'm working my way regularly through the circulating library, reading about two chapters of every first volume…*

1919 A War Memorial porch by C.W. Oldrid Scott is added to St. Paul's, and in 1920 Temple Lushington Moore, an important late Victorian architect, advises the removal of the gallery so the capacity is reduced to 450 places. Charles Powell carries out the lovely ceiling decoration, 1927-36.

1934 Sandgate's Public Library warmed by coal, opens in the Reading Room on the first floor of the former Volunteer Fire Station and, in 1974, KCC takes control under Local Government reorganisation. In 1982 the Library moves to modern premises beneath the council flats for the elderly on the site of the James Morris dwellings, on the High Street. The Sandgate Heritage Trust Ltd. (Reg. Charity 287281) succeeds in purchasing the historic building from KCC and maintaining it for community use. The Sandgate Society (founded 1962) rents the Old Engine Room as HQ and forms a focal point in village life.

1944 KCC becomes the controlling authority for school finance and administration, and the National School becomes known as the Sandgate Church of England Primary School. At the end of World War II the evacuee pupils return from the Wye Valley area to somewhat dilapidated premises and overflow into four 'Caravan classrooms' on the site of the James Morris dwellings.

1953 The Fynmore family dedicate a window in the Parish Church to the memory of R.J. Fynmore (1839-1920) Lt.Col. of the 1st Cinque Ports Artillery Volunteers, and a great Sandgate administrator. He was also an antiquary who meticulously and lovingly documented Sandgate life. The window depicting two events in the life of St. Paul is in the South Chancel. He is buried in St. Martin's churchyard, Horn Street.

1970 Fifty thousand pounds of public funds are squandered on the reinforcement of foundations for an alternative Primary School in Golden Valley, on ground well-known to be unstable. Ultimately the site is abandoned.

1972 In October, the children move uphill to the new County Primary School on Coolinge Lane and the future of the 1866 school premises is at stake. Its conversion to a larger Sandgate Public Library is turned down and Lord Radnor's agents intend to demolish it and reclaim 'the deeded land' for redevelopment. Quickly a Grade II listing, agreed by the DoE, forestalls its destruction.

1976 Developers apply for Scheduled Monument Consent and The Sandgate Society, among others, is fiercely opposed. A Local Inquiry follows (23 March) and the Inspector decides that *Public interest is best served by permitting partial development.* Meanwhile, the old School has been used as an Antiques Centre, and two tall town houses are wedged in the playground.

c.1986 A caring, local resident rescues the historic School building, respects its special features and converts it most sensitively into 6 flats. Thankfully this beloved landmark, in the Conservation Area, remains a tribute to James Morris who spared nothing to endow Sandgate's children with a place of use and beauty.

1992 Sandgate's Church of St Paul and St. George's, Folkestone, become a United Benefice.

1998 Among recent vicars the Rev. Clinton Davis, who started out in criminal law resigns after ten years in Sandgate to become a Prison Chaplain. His successor, the Rev. David Makepeace, organises a Youth Club (8-12 years) among plans for revitalisation. Teulon's Church is showing signs of wear, but there are plans and visions for the future.

Sandgate's Public Library (moved 1982) set below pavement level, has undergone repeated flooding and faces permanent closure. Local councillors, The Sandgate Society and concerned residents exert pressure and, finally, the authorities agree to resite the High Street entrance. By July the essential Library is fully restored, to the benefit and joy of young and old.

Left: *Wesleyan church, demolished 1970's*
Right: *Soldier's Home (1879) Jubilee clock is later removed to Chichester Hall.*
Collection Alan Taylor

Coastal Watch

Coastguard Station rebuilt 1896, western end near Esplanade. Alex Todd

DUNGENESS BAY, in the lawless days of smuggling and privateering, is a hotbed for the covert landing and transport of contraband by daring gangs of smugglers out to defy the Excise men. During the Napoleonic Wars, their traffic is tolerated for, Sir John Moore finds, they and their relations in Flushing can be useful as spies. John Gough remembers a well-organised gang in the village – a bold and hardy set of men, operating under pseudonyms, their favourite haunt being the 'Fleur de Lis' tavern. Sandgate is well served with tunnels and cellars. To guard the shore a Watch House stands just west of the Castle (Radnor lease 1798) and an 1843 survey of Shorncliffe Ordnance Ground marks a narrow site as 'Coastguard'.

1864 The Board of Customs (est. 1822) erects a permanent Sandgate Coastguard Station near the Esplanade. A 99-year Radnor lease (1862) shows it on the site of the Marine Hotel, previously the residence of Sir John Shaw and, briefly, of Sir John Moore his tenant. Here, the Coastguards act as naval auxiliaries, their duty being to protect the Revenue, save life, salvage wrecks and patrol the shore.

1876 Miss Hannah de Rothschild presents Sandgate with a Lifeboat and Boathouse in memory of her father, Baron Mayer de Rothschild 15 years MP for the District. It stands at the western end of Sandgate, an extraordinary Gothic structure *more like a Nonconformist tabernacle than a Boathouse* as Jocelyn Brooke recalls in *The Goose Cathedral* (1950), hinting at the Teahouse it later becomes, with geese pecking on the lawns.

SHIPWRECKS, indeed, are numerous along this often merciless Bay. In westerly gales or fog, schooners, ironclads, steamboats founder and heroic rescues follow. They are a tragic, haunting scene to those on shore. In 1825, John Gough a small boy of seven, beholds the wreck of an East Indiaman *The Lady of Calcutta* in which 790 passengers, returning troops and seamen perish: *For weeks after I saw in my dreams the hair of women floating on the water as I had seen it in reality when the boats went out to fetch the scores of bodies, or they were washed ashore.* In 1878 two German ships the *Grosser Kurfurst* and the *Köenig Wilhem* veer to avoid a Norwegian barque, and collide while on exercises in the Channel. The former sinks within eight minutes leaving 600 men and boys floundering in the sea. Lifeboats and fishing vessels are able to save 218; the rest perish and finders of bodies on Sandgate beach are rewarded with a pound. In January 1883 the iron sailing ship *Plassey* is beached off Sandgate.

1891 Gales blow with unprecedented violence. Among vessels in distress, the 2000 ton full-rigged *Benvenue* breaks from a tug and sinks 300 yards off Wellington Terrace while the crew takes refuge in the rigging. *The lifeboat now the Coastguards try to launch/To rescue*

those poor fellows on the mast/They fail; the liquid mountains hurl them back/ Nor can a rocket face the roaring blast (Verse 4, C.H.1891). As a small boy, Victor Foley of Wellington Terrace, witnesses the horror. His epic painting done in later life, hangs in Sandgate's Public Library. The November gales of 1893 reach 90 miles an hour and the Sandgate Lifeboat is launched 60 times to aid vessels in distress.

1896 The Coastguard's Area HQ is severely damaged in the 1893 landslip. The 5th Earl of Radnor grants his lessees, the Lords Commissioners of the Admiralty, a licence to *rebuild the Station after making good the breaches in the seawall.*

1902 H.G. Wells in his *Sea Lady* fantasy, pooh-poohs local smuggling as an old man's tale of forty years past: *The existing Coastguard is a sacrifice to a vain superstition.*

1925 The Coastguard Act transfers the Service to the Commissioners of Works (later Board of Trade) which, in 1932, auctions all but five of the remaining leases to the private sector.

1961 On expiry of the Radnor Lease of 1862, the last Sandgate Coastguards, whose duty now is search and rescue, are transferred to East Cliff Folkestone until 1990. Several moves later, in 1996 the Service (Department of Trade) is based at the Ambulance Station, Cheriton, when modern communications technology replaces official 'Look-outs' excepting that at Dover.

1996 A uniformed contingent of regular and auxiliary Coastguards from Folkestone and Dover together with residents, celebrate the Centenary of the rebuilding of the now private Coastguard row. The old Coastguard Ensign briefly flys again above the former Look-out; Derek St Clair-Stannard MBE, son of the former Chief Officer (d.1931) cuts the Centenary cake; the Regional Controller, Derek Smith, presents a commemorative plaque and the band of T/S Invicta Sea Cadet Corps enlivens the feasting.

Wreck of the three-masted BENVENUE November 1891. Coastguards attempt rescue with rocket apparatus and field gun

Above: *Sandgate beach looking east. Castle on left, bathing machine to right.*
Below: *Sandgate village bordering post-road west to Hythe. Castle on left; Martello Towers on heights.*
Watercolours by Lt.Col W.H. Ford c.1811. William Drummond, London ©

People and Pleasures

SEA AIR AND SEABATHING are deemed highly beneficial in the treatment of nervous and bodily ills and, in the mid 18th century, nature's 'remedy' gives rise to fashionable resorts – Margate, Ramsgate, Hastings and Brighton – and others round the coast of England. By the end of the century, Sandgate's shipyards have declined; apart from some boatbuilders, fisherfolk and washerwomen mainly east of the Castle, the pebble beach is empty. Sandgate, small but ideally located, looks to the future as an elegant resort for invalids, and persons of rank and quality.

Romford's (1805-6) the earliest of Pocket Guides to the area, is eloquent...*Sandgate can claim at least an equal degree of admiration to any watering place in England.* The *Kentish Gazette* (1809) assures the intending visitor: *the seabathing here is of the greatest perfection, as the waters are pure*...describes the varied pleasant walks and rides, and *its cliffs of easy ascent commanding a beautiful view of the British Channel, the undulating line of the French coast in the distance, the whole of the luxuriant Level of Romney Marsh and parts of neighbouring Sussex.* The earliest Inns include 'The Trotting Horse', the 'New Inn' run by Richard Marsh and the 'Good Intent' (later York Cottage) where Sir John Moore lodges his mother and sister. Public Houses include the 'Fleur de Luce' reputedly the haunt of smugglers.

In 1816, W.Tiffen publishes a set of five romantic aquatints of the district including Sandgate, engraved by J. Jeakes. *(Mellon Coll. Virginia).* Fussell, in his *Journey Round the Coast of Kent* (1818) admits there is no theatre *but the scenery which nature presents on all sides is grand, romantic and delightful – here are neither balls nor concerts; but the diversified beauties of the country around will afford ample amusement amidst the tranquility which soothes the mind and invigorates the body.* He invites the invalid to 'shun the rank city' and seek the purer air of this peaceful shore. But Sandgate's very 'smallness' breeds a genteel informality and Thomas Purday's elegant Library and Reading Room (c.1800) becomes the hub of social life.

At all times, Sandgate has a quality which endears it to writers, artists, 'eccentrics' among others. Their experiences help to define it and the history of the area comes to life.

1789 PHILIP THICKNESSE (1719-92) polemist and 'private eye' known as *Dr. Viper* is perhaps the first eccentric to settle in Sandgate towards the end of his querulous life. His third wife, authoress and musician Ann Ford (1737-1824), describes his latest unconventional move to a deserted Barn in the small fishing village of Sandgate. Standing on the beach itself, it presented every advantage in point of situation and prospect *but it was nothing better than a tobacco warehouse, unshapely in point of form which had been abandoned by the manufacturer and could be purchased for a trifle.* His 'creative genius' sets to work. A large glass window is inserted into the gable-end facing the sea, opening upon a prospect at once noble and sublime. A suite of bedchambers is produced as if by enchantment, Ann's drawings adorn a parlour while, to crown it all *a guilded crescent placed on the roof, gives an appearance of taste and whimsicality to the whole.* Thicknesse is a Francophile, no matter the Revolutionary unrest. The sight of Boulogne and its steeples through his glass, lures them over. He dies in his postchaise in November 1792 and is buried in Boulogne.

Above left: *William Wilberforce MP.*
Right: *Sarah Siddons by Sir William Beechey (detail) 1793.* Courtesy National Portrait Gallery
Below left: *H.G. Wells, 1901.* Folkestone Library. Right: *James Morris Esq. of Encombe*

1790 SARAH SIDDONS (1755-1831) foremost tragic actress of the day, returns from a visit to France where her daughters are at school. After a very rough crossing to Dover, she makes haste to Sandgate. On 2 August she writes to Lady Harcourt…*it is the most agreeable seaplace, excepting those on the Devonshire coast, I ever saw. Perhaps agreeable is a bad word, for the country is much more sublime than beautiful. We have tremendous cliffs overhanging and frowning on the foaming sea, which is very often so saucy and tempestuous as to deserve frowning on…Here are little neat lodgings, and good wholesome provisions. Perhaps they would not suit a great countess, as our friend Mr. Mason* [poet and dramatist] *has it, but a little great actress is more easily accommodated. I'm afraid it will grow larger, though, and then adieu to the comforts of retirement. At present the place cannot contain above twenty or thirty strangers, I should think. I have bathed four times, and I believe I shall persevere on. Sir Lucas Pepys says my disease is entirely nervous.*

1794 ANN RADCLIFFE (1764-1823) novelist (incl. *Mysteries of Udolpho*) passes through pristine Sandgate: *the white, new village straggling along the beach on each side of the wide road, wide free and pleasant* she calls it in her *Journey made in the Summer of 1794.*

1804 Lt.Gen.JOHN MOORE writes to Thomas Creevey (27 August) : *My situation here becomes daily more irksome, and I am almost reduced to wish for peace. I am tired of confinement, without the occupation of war.* He is renting Sir John Shaw's villa for three gns a week (later, the site of the Marine Hotel and then the Coastguard Area HQ). The monotony is broken by the arrival of the Duke of York who, as Commander in Chief of the British Army, comes to review the troops. He stays at the 'Good Intent' (known later as the 'Duke of York') and faces the lonely prospect of *two whole nights before I shall clasp my darling* (Mary Ann Clarke) *in my arms.* Lady Hester Stanhope (1776-1839) might be glimpsed in her scarlet habit riding over from Walmer Castle, *à l'amazone,* to see her brother Charles, and sharing his hero-worship for Moore his Commander. Balls are fortnightly events for the officers, friends and families with marriageable daughters.

1806 JOHN 4th EARL OF DARNLEY (1767-1831) of Cobham Hall, a Whig, is an active promoter of Catholic Emancipation and Electoral Reform. He purchases an extensive tract of hillside just north of the Post-road and builds Belle Vue, his marine villa (rebuilt 1852 as Enbrook House). He surrounds it with woodlands which, in time, enhance the village and he is the first in the region to introduce N.American species, ilex, camelia and exotic shrubs. In 1830, HRH Prince Leopold (soon to be King of the Belgians) pays him a visit and orders a cutter from John Lowes.

1812 WILLIAM WILBERFORCE MP (1756-1833) has just resigned his Yorkshire seat after 32 years in parliament, before becoming Member for the pocket borough of Bramber. He brings his wife Barbara and five children aged 5-14 years old, in search of quiet to restore his health, and time for reading, writing and the enjoyment of nature. *Sandgate he writes is one of the creations of modern English opulence. A number of very comfortable houses for warm or even moderate weather, with a library, a warm bath, and other appendages. The country by far the most picturesque of any sea coast I have seen in the south of England.* He picnics with his family in the Cherry Gardens or on Caesar's Camp, and takes them to Dover to see Congreve's 'rockets'.

In the Summers of 1813-14 Wilberforce is back, intensely busy on Slave Trade matters while enjoying with his family *the overflowing bounty of the Almighty.*

1813 MME. D'ARBLAY (Fanny Burney) in September, after ten years seclusion, finally escapes from France. On a visit to her brother Charles and family in Sandgate, she is introduced to William Wilberforce coming out of Folkestone Church: *The Ramparts & Martellos around us became naturally our theme & Mr. Wilberforce proposed showing them to me.* A fascinating four-hour walk and talk then followed. *In contemplating the opposite & alas hostile shore which to our Fanny's eye, at least, was visible I could not forbear wafting over to it a partial blessing nor refuse myself beseeching one from Mr. Wilberforce...*Her husband, General d'Arblay is still immured in France.

1814 MARIANNE FRANCIS (1790-1832) a niece of Fanny Burney has come under Wilberforce's wing in whose hospitable mansion (the original Knoll House) she is to spend six weeks as companion to his children. In September, Marianne writes to Dr. Johnson's old friend, Mrs (Thrale) Piozzi: *This place is admirably sheltered from the wind; good bathing, delightful walks, a fine sea, & the French cliffs on the opposite shore visible to the naked eye. I long to ferry over. If you ever want a quiet sea-place, dear Mrs Piozzi, do think of Sandgate.* Writing from Bath in October 1820, Mrs Piozzi tells Fanny Burney d'Arblay: *my family are all gone to Sandgate for the purpose of bathing in the sea this wonderfully beautiful October and were you not detained in London...I should wish you there too.* (Her daughter Sophia Hoare dies in Sandgate 8 November 1824).

c.1819 HENRY DAWKINS (1765-1852) a former MP and Commissioner of Woods Forests and Land Revenues (1810-1832), buys an old farm on the slopes above Sandgate, and little by little acquires a scrubby tract of surplus land from the War Department. Here, with his wife Augusta (daughter of General Sir Henry Clinton first Governor of New York) he builds a handsome residence called Encombe. He lays out woods and shady walks, lending in time a verdant beauty also to the village.

1832 MARY SHELLEY (1797-1851) Author of *Frankenstein* etc. takes up lodgings to avoid the cholera epidemic now menacing London. Trelawney asks her to care for his daughter, teach her housekeeping and engage her mind.

1823 MRS FRANCES LEIGH of Barn House, Lord Byron's aunt, dies 19 October and is buried at St. Martin's, Horn Street.

1843 ELIZABETH FRY (1780-1845) Quaker and Prison Reformer stays a while in Sandgate for her failing health: *I find myself here in a lovely place by the sea, the air delightful, and the house [on the Lower Road] pleasant. If it please my Holy Helper, may He soon see meet to heal me.*

1848 ANGELA BURDETT COUTTS (1814-1906) philanthropist daughter of eminent Bankers, takes Farleigh House on Sandgate Esplanade for the season, within polite range of Walmer Castle and her adored friend the Duke of Wellington, Lord Warden of the Cinque Ports. He rides over to Sandgate, stops briefly at the Marine Hotel where he chats to Saxby, a local pensioner named about their Peninsular experiences, and slips him a sovereign. Dickens also writes to 'dear Miss Coutts' (21 September 1847) at this address.

1852 THE DUKE OF WELLINGTON (1769-1852) takes the train to Folkestone (2 September) and sets out on foot to visit his old friend, John Wilson Croker, (politician and essayist) at 3 Radnor Terrace, Folkestone: *I was told,* writes the Duke *it was half a mile; then that it was a mile; it was three miles across the valley, through the town down the hill, then up a steep hill.* But Croker is not at home. He receives Wellington two days later little knowing the Duke has only ten more days to live. He describes Mrs Croker on his arm, descending the steps from the house.

UNDER A DEED OF ASSIGNMENT.

[L]IBRARY AND READING ROOMS,
SANDGATE.

A CATALOGUE
OF THE WHOLE OF THE VALUABLE

LENDING LIBRARY,
CONSISTING OF UPWARDS OF

[5],000 STANDARD VOLUMES,
Novels, Biography, History, Travels,

HASTED'S HISTORY OF KENT;
BOOKBINDER'S STANDING PRESS,

Superior Full-toned Pianoforte,
TOGETHER WITH THE WHOLE
... HOUSEHOLD

J. MARSH,
FISHMONGER,
SANDGATE.
Lobsters, Crabs, Shrimps and Prawns fresh every day during the Season.
BEST NATIVE OYSTERS.
Pleasure Boats for Hire by the day or hour

Sandgate Sept. 3rd 1860
Messrs Jenner & Co

Dr. to M P Valyer
Corn Factor & Coal Merchant,
Hay & Straw. Livery Stables
AGENT FOR FIRE & LIFE INSURANCE.
Two Loads Coals 15/9 1 11 6

T. WOODMAN

Families supplied on the most reasonable Terms.
No business transacted on Sundays.
Butcher
SANDGATE.

EMILY GRIMWOOD.
CONFECTIONER,
Pastry Cook, Fancy Bread & Biscuit Baker.
DEALER IN
CORN, HAY, STRAW, SEEDS &c.
SANDGATE.
Dinners & Evening Parties supplied

SANDGATE 185*4*
Mr Wm Jenner

BOUGHT OF HENRY COTTMAN
Tea Dealer, Grocer & Oilman,

Fruits, Spices, Pickles & Sauces, British Wines, &c.
Wax, Sperm Composite and other Candles
Dealer in China, Glass & Earthenware
HOUSE AGENT.

Feby 6.	*28 lb Sugar*	*11 8*
11.	*Chocolate*	*1 2*
15.	*1. Butter / Dutch*	*1 2*
	1 3/4 Cheese	*1 0½*
		15 0½

Recd ... 10

SELECT FAMILY ARTICLES,
ESTABLISHED 1837.
PREPARED AND SOLD BY
JENNER & CO.,
DISPENSING AND FAMILY CHEMISTS,
SANDGATE, KENT.

Sandgate as a Health Resort,

WITH PARTICULAR REFERENCE TO

"BEACH ROCKS" CONVALESCENT HOME.

OUR OMNIBUS.

1858 - 1914 MUSIC HALL NIGHTS: Sandgate in the mid-Victorian era is to all intents and purposes a sedate and well-ordered place. By day the visitors set the tone; by night however, the military, sailors, fisherfolk and others set the pace. Over a dozen beerhalls and taverns abound to cope with their 'transcendent thirst'. With around 5000 men at the Camp, a 25-strong army piquet patrols the village where, on Saturday nights, skirmishes and pitched battles are known to break out.

Entertainment flourishes. In 1858 Bob Rigden, enterprising proprietor of The Bricklayer's Arms in the High St. builds a Concert Room and Music Hall at the back of his premises, locally known as THE BRICKS. This is the start of 50 years live and varied entertainment until the silent stars of the silver screen take over. The high, gas-lit Hall (65 x 25ft) is hung with three resplendent glass chandeliers and others light the aisles. The opening evening makes a 'splash' with a pianist and vocalist, a ballad singer, a negro melodist, and a Miss Anne Zelleta fresh from London performs a ballet.

Later billings include Belle Elmore, Crippen's wife and a retired hangman named Berry. At the request of Sandgate's vicar, his morbid 'act' is withdrawn. Lillie North, R.W. Bentley and Clara Nesbitt (13 times) draw crowds from far and near. Able managers include Charles Chaplin Sr. (1890) and George Leybourne, son of 'Champagne Charlie' (1904). In January 1895, Oscar Wilde's *A Woman of No Importance* amuses the locals and in 1897, the Barron Brothers, pioneers of the moving image, rage of Paris and London, are engaged at great expense.

Charles Coburn (1852-1945) famed for his song *The Man who Broke the Bank at Monte Carlo* (1886), gets his real start in Sandgate. He arrives one dark Sunday night in December 1875 with fourpence in his pocket and unsure where to lay his head: *I had some diifficulty in finding my way along the sea road, and the roar of waves on the shingle quite near me, but scarcely visible, had a peculiar effect upon me, producing a feeling of awe and mystery and a longing for company.* He knocks on the wrong door and meets up with a couple of negro performers. One of them, Chirgwin 'the white-eyed Kaffir' is the cleverest all-round artiste he would ever meet, and they are friends for life. During his extended 5-week stint in Sandgate, Charlie works up a song in praise of the Coastguard suitably clad by Chief Officer. But it does not 'go'. *GO – not likely,* says a friend, *YOU praising the Coastguard when they are all bloomin' SMUGGLERS about here.*

Proprietors change and so does the name: to the Alexandra Hotel and Music Hall in 1867; to Maltby's Mansion of Mirth, modernised in 1891 and Hill's Hall of Hilarity in 1897 – but more often it is known as THE ALHAMBRA or simply THE BRICKS. Slowly, the silent films take over. Ironically, just two months before the outbreak of World War I with an influx of new recruits to Kitchener's Army, the Music Hall closes its doors for good. For a brief spell it serves as a Canadian YMCA and the Rex Cinema comes into being after the war is over.

* * *

1871 THE CENSUS RETURN for Sandgate has almost doubled since 1841, from 979 to near on 2200 souls, including 54 officially in Folkestone Township.

Not surprisingly, Sandgate has risen in numbers and repute. Climate, scenery and charm continue to attract the discerning visitor, and good hotels such as the Royal Norfolk and the Royal Kent (formerly the 'New Inn') are in demand. Lodging houses and elegant villas on the Undercliffe, Radnor Cliff and Esplanade are rented for the summer season. James Field, a London architect of note, has also built spacious seafront homes east of the Castle to Castle Green, on land acquired in 1839 from Lord Radnor. Enterprising citizens set out to cater for every comfort and pleasure. The Devonshire Rooms (on Devonshire Terrace) provide entertainment; horses, carriages, bathing machines are for hire, and warm salt-water baths are popular. Business on the Broadway (High Street) is brisk, with tailors, drapers, bootmakers, wine & spirit merchants, coal merchant, and provisions of every sort. Every great house holds a history and every host and hostess attracts a political or artistic coterie.

1874 EMPRESS EUGENIE visits General Hankey at Cliff House.

1884 The Misses Reilly who have taken over Encombe (1883) throw open their lovely grounds for a Bazaar with bands and sideshows, to raise money for the building of the Volunteer Fire Station and Reading Room above. On the occasion of the Golden Jubilee (1897), the children of Sandgate parade in fancy dress through the beflagged village, and enjoy a glorious day in the Encombe grounds.

1887-8 JOHN RUSKIN (1819-1900) who revels in seas and skies, is staying in Devonshire Terrace lodgings. He writes, 19 February 1888 to Kate Greenaway: *This is the dismallest day I've ever seen at Sandgate, but I'm cheering it up by trying to fancy tea at Frognal…and remembering the teas of old times.*

1893 PRINCE AND PRINCESS LOUIS OF BATTENBERG with their children are staying at the Undercliffe. *They have won golden opinions from the inhabitants of Sandgate with whom they mingle quite freely.*

1898-1910 H.G. WELLS (1866-1946) visiting New Romney as a sick man, chances upon Sandgate. Late in 1898, he rents Beach Cottage on Granville Parade, where the waves break over the roof and the shrimps, so he says, land 'thwack' on the oilcloth. He writes to H[ubert] B[land]…*whether I shall buy a home or build a house or fly unto the uttermost parts of the Earth and howl DAMN, no man can tell…but the Lord has forgot to stir up my insides as usual, and I AM GETTING BETTER.* In March 1899, Wells takes a 3-year lease on Arnold House (20 Castle Road) while, as a man far ahead of his times, he commissions C.F.A. Voysey (RIBA Gold Medallist 1940) to design Spade House on one of the finest sites in Sandgate. Wells calls him *that pioneer of the escape from the small snobbish villa residence to the bright and comfortable pseudo-cottage.* The lower floor offers plenty of space for bicycles: *when I see an adult on a bicycle, I have hope for the human race.* The hydraulic lift to the Leas passes the house by viaduct; he calls it his 'moving staircase'.

Renewed in health and spirit, Wells raises a family and produces 17 novels, and other stories and studies during his 12-year stay. They include *Kipps, Ann Veronica* and *The Sea Lady,* a fantasy on Sandgate's fish-tailed temptress. If Sandgate is good for Wells, so Wells is good for Sandgate. England's literary lights are at his door – George Gissing, Arnold Bennett, Anthony Hope, Sir James Barrie, G.K. Chesterton, A.E.W. Mason, John Galsworthy, Hilaire Belloc – and Fabians such as Hubert Bland, the Webbs, Graham Wallas and Bernard Shaw.

FORD MADOX FORD in 1938 remembers…*the sunlight over Sandgate and the sea, and Mr. Wells and I descending the steep brae that goes down from the hutments of Shorncliffe Camp to the narrow High Street, whose outer row of houses was so close to the sea that in great westerly gales the Indiamen going ashore used to poke their bowsprits through the windows. For that was the landscape of my childhood's school and Mr. Well's 'Sea Lady'.* Josef Conrad, Henry James, Stephen Crane and W.H. Hudson dwelt within a radius of five to thirty miles of Spade House *so it was not to be wondered at if we lived rather in each other's pockets.*

Spade House, renamed Bay House, changes hands. In 1927 the Hon. Gerald Montagu (3rd son of 1st Lord Swaythling) and his family live there. After World War II, Spade House becomes a vegetarian hotel and then a nursing home. In 1966, Sandgate celebrates the centenary of Wells' birth. Among other events Frank Wells, his younger son, plants a tree on the triangle in Castle Road. On the 50th anniversary of his death in 1996, Reginald Turnill leads a 'Walk-about' and Martin Wells, a grandson, unveils a plaque.

Below: *Encombe House, south aspect c.1924*

1908 YOUTH activities are an important element in Sandgate life. The formation of the 1st Sandgate Scouts Troop by Major Tuke, provides a constructive and often adventurous outlet for their energies; it helps form character and purpose, also a care for those in need of help. Fred Moore, who joins as a youngster of 11, rises in 1937 to become an inspiring Scoutmaster of the 2nd Sandgate Troop which wins high praise. By 1956, hard work and enthusiasm raises £2000 in small sums to build their own quarters at the Undercliffe. In 1976, Fred (local Shoe Repairer Extraordinary) earns scouting's highest award The Silver Wolf and, after his retirement, the BEM in 1983. To his pride and joy, many a grateful scout keeps in touch; many have done well in life including Andrew Brownsword (Bath) a millionaire publisher.

Likewise the Sea Cadets (formed 1942) run their 'ship' T.S. Invicta in the 1845 National School quarters in Castle Road, acquired in 1947. In an atmosphere of comradeship, girls and boys of 10-18 learn nautical tradition, modern day skills and technology, discipline and teamwork which can lead to the Duke of Edinburgh's award scheme, and prepare in general for adult life. They run a splendid Band.

1912 LILLA, COUNTESS OF CHICHESTER of Enbrook House dies 8 December 1911. Residents form a Committee to decide on a lasting memorial in recognition of her many services and benefactions to the village. Sir Philip Sassoon and his sister Sybil preside at the meeting at Shorncliffe Lodge.

1914/18 The Chichester Memorial Hall and Working Men's Club opens as a handsome community centre in the heart of Sandgate and displays the ornate Jubilee Clock (removed on the sale of the Gough Soldiers Institute). The hall is built on a semi-derelict site, entirely by public subscription. By Indenture 1 February 1918, the Chichester Hall Committee transfers the land and property to the Sandgate Urban District Council and successors who, with a Committee of five members, shall maintain the Hall and permit its use for public, political and religious meetings or meetings of other bodies in the town.

Actor/Manager Sir Squire Bancroft admits to a new role when laying the foundation stone in 1913. An imposing figure with a bush of white hair and a black-ribboned monocle, he is President of the Actors' Association on the death of Sir Henry Irving (1905). He lives at Underlea (Lower Sandgate Road) and is one of the stage and screen fraternity who, over the years, are attracted to Sandgate – George Arliss, David Tomlinson, Alec McCowen CBE and Denis de Marne. In his boyhood, Daniel Thorndike and his family occupy West Wedge, West Sandgate west of Folkestone as they liked to say. After the War he too makes his name in the Theatre.

In 1990, organised by Geoffrey Edmunds (Chairman of The Sandgate Society) and local citizens, a Charitable Trust is quickly formed to take over this Village Hall when Shepway Council are about to sell it off. The Trust ensures its continued use for meetings, lectures, classes and other forms of recreational activity with the object of improving the conditions of local life. Students at Folkestone Girls School enliven the walls with Sandgate scenes in painted roundels, inspired by David Embry, their art teacher. The ground floor continues to be leased to the Men's Club, with billiard tables, darts and other amenities.

c.1913 MRS B.M. CROKER lives at No.5 Radnor Cliff till her death in 1920. Known as Mary Bithia Sheppard, she has written 22 romances, one of which is dramatised.

1922 ENCOMBE reaches its social heyday in the hands of Ralph Hilton Philipson, a wealthy colliery owner and director of the North Eastern Railway and his 2nd wife Mabel who prefers the name of Maya.

This enchanted site has passed through many hands. On the death of Henry Dawkins in 1852, the estate is sold to James Morris, Director and one of three serving Governors (1847-48) of the Bank of England. On his death in 1882, the Reilly sisters Hester Jane and Theodosia take it over though unstable ground has rendered the house uninhabitable. On their death it passes to a niece, Mrs Matilda Bell who employs Sir Ernest George to rebuild the house. Her daughter, Maude Lady Sackville West inherits it, and then her son Edward who becomes the well-known writer on music and recordings. But, just 19, he chooses not to retain it.

Maya commissions Basil Ionides FRIBA to transform the house into a white, arcaded Mediterranean-style villa and week-end paradise. Widely travelled, Maya is a collector of beautiful artifacts and fascinating people who come to adorn her salon. Algernon Blackwood and Lord Thomson are among the elect. Maude Ffoulkes, the journalist, recalls the enchantment. She tells of *Mary Borden's charm, Mrs Somerset Maugham's soignée perfection, Julie Le Gallienne's outspokenness.* She hears Sir Denison Ross singing Schubert liede in the great white music room and Harry Ainley declaiming verse in soul-stirring tones. In 1928, Edith Wharton passes through Sandgate after a visit to the Norton's at Lamb House, Rye.

Algernon Blackwood, writer; Lord Thomson of Fleet, newspaper magnate; Henry Ainley, Actor/Manager; Sir Denison Ross, orientalist; Mary Borden (Lady Spears) novelist.

Among the beech and chestnut-shaded lawns George Punnett, benign spirit and devoted gardener for 40 years, tends the lilies, roses, camelias and the sea of delphiniums glimpsed through white arches. The Water Gardens are a special feature. Cascades and pools, paved with brick and flanked with espalier pears, are designed to drain spring-water from the treacherous hillside. (Sandgate Laundry, at the foot, makes good use of it). Ralph Philipson dies in 1928. After World War II, the Abbey National acquires the deserted estate for a staff holiday home. By the mid-1960's, the nightingales have fled. Developers have massacred the trees, wrecked the Water Gardens and carved up the estate. In 1978 the pathetic, crumbling Encombe House burns down in mysterious circumstances.

1935 The Rex Cinema closes after some 'fiddle' with the takings. The springs are coming through the seats, gales whistle through the cracks and the screen trembles to the crash of waves. Watching Lon Chaney and Lillian Gish is a haunting experience. Post-War, Rayner's Beach Club takes over the site.

1948 JOCELYN BROOKE (1908-1966) soldier and writer recalls his childhood in the Elham Valley and at No.9 Radnor Cliff: *My memories [of Sandgate] are bathed in the keen, windy light of spring mornings, a seaside gaiety and brilliance haunted by the thud of waves on the shingle and the tang of seaweed...* During the winter, so he writes, the village becomes *a Land of Lost Content the symbol of a happiness which would only be renewed again in the spring.* As a botanist, he is struck by the many plants – Henbane, Horned Poppy, Bristly Oxtongue and Tree-mallow – common to Sandgate and to the cliffs by the Adriatic where he is stationed during the War.

1966 The Little Theatre run by Folkestone and Hythe Operatic and Dramatic Society (founded 1913) opens in the converted Congregational Chapel almost opposite the old Alhambra on the High Street. Here, FHODS and other groups stage year-round and often award winning shows. The Theatre seats just over 100 people.

1977 Sandgate honours the Queen. The Sandgate Silver Jubilee Committee sets up a week-long series of events for young and old. It starts with a Thanksgiving Service in the Church of St. Paul and ends with an Open Boat angling competition off Granville Parade. Members of the Sandgate Society design and erect the decorations which gain third prize in the *Illustrated London News* contest for the 'best-dressed village'.

1984 To celebrate the Centenary of the former Volunteer Fire Station on the High St. a week of festivity begins with a candle-lit supper in the lovely, panelled Reading Room on the upper floor. Guest of honour is Peter Fynmore, whose grandfather Lt.Col. R.J. Fynmore was 13 times Chairman of the Sandgate Board of Health and of the Urban District Council till 1905. It also marks the success of the Sandgate Heritage Trust Ltd. (Reg.Charity), specially set up to raise funds (£18,100) and save this beloved village landmark when KCC are intent on selling it off. The Sandgate Society is thus enabled to rent the old Engine Room as their HQ, and as a heritage centre and rendezvous for residents and visitors. Patrons of the Trust include Sir John Betjeman, and Dame Professor Sheila Sherlock MD who grew up in Sandgate on Devonshire Terrace.

1990's Despite the growth and pace of modern life, Sandgate is a place to be leisurely. A bus service and two large carparks make it easy to stop and explore its leafy, well-marked footpaths with sweeping views across the Channel, or take a stroll along the beachfront. Formal recreation space is limited except for the grassy playground on Military Road which once had tennis courts and bowling green. But at the western extremity of Sandgate Esplanade, the Royal Military Canal (a Scheduled Ancient Monument) conceived as an obstacle to a Napoleonic invasion, begins its scenic 25-mile course across Romney Marsh to Cliff End in Sussex. The Saxon Shoreway, alongside, forms a pleasant walk to Hythe.

The seashore offers its delights. Sunbathing, swimming and water sports such as rowing and windsurfing are popular. Regattas are held off Granville Parade where the trophy-laden Folkestone Rowing Club (founded 1852) is proof of local prowess. Sea-angling is good and national contests take place along the shoreline. And Sandgate is quite 'with it'. Though it has hardly a grain of sand to its name, the Victorians might have blinked at the lovely naked bodies which, instead, adorn the beaches.

The village itself has much to offer. Antique and bric-à-brac shops along the High St. are fun to browse and a magnet for home and overseas buyers. There are several gourmet restaurants, and a long-established Fish and Chip shop. Friendly, old-world pubs such as the 'Providence' and 'Ship Inn', and the 'Clarendon' on Brewers Hill offer snacks and meals. Notable are two quality hotels, the Sandgate Hotel with Terrasse Restaurant on the Esplanade, and the Royal Norfolk Hotel close to the Church; also there are some well-appointed B&B's.

At the culmination of the 20th century, Sandgate's pleasures gain a new dimension – the quick and easy access to the Continent by way of modern Ferry Services and the Channel Tunnel.

Above: 1829: *Post road through Sandgate, shipwright's cottages (c.1773) to fore and Chapel of Ease (1822) close by.* Below: 1998: *Same cottages; to North, SAGA HQ takes shape*

GRAND EVENING CONCERT

GIVEN BY Mrs. MARK H. JUDGE,

(CASTLE GLEN, SANDGATE).

In aid of the Sandgate Landslip Relief Fund.

Town Hall Folkestone, Saturday, April 1st, 1893, at 8 p.m.

Environment

SANDGATE PEOPLE are alive to the beauties and the hazards that surround them. They are weatherwatchers, coastwatchers by instinct; listeners to the ocean's changing beat. Yet, they are lulled by pearly days of calm until a merciless storm or North Sea surge play havoc with vessels and sea defences at the deepest indent of Dungeness Bay. Survivors, since centuries, of the *outrageous flowing, surges and course of the sea,** landwards they are also watchful for signs of subsidence and earthslip, well documented in *A Survey of Coastal Landslides of Kent* (1965) by Professor J.N. Hutchinson late of Imperial College, London.

Living as they do between the devil and the deep blue sea, Sandgate people are aware of the complex geological strata – water absorbent and permeable – which interact beneath the lovely hills to the North. Locally, the slopes are capped by the Folkestone beds which weigh upon the soft Sandgate beds of sandy clay. Forming a slip plane (NW/SE) these overlay the hard Hythe beds, mainly limestone and hassock. Beneath these lie uneven bands of Atherfield clay with the hard Weald clay at their base. Offshore reefs of ragstone indicate the Hythe beds, mostly taken for sea defences, houses, garden walls and even the Castle itself. Seaweed covered gault or slipe is visible at low tide near the toe of the slip.

This unstable terrain, as records show, is affected by coast erosion, loss of toe-weighting, Spring tides and periods of exceptionally heavy rainfall.

1801 **LANDSLIPS 19th C.** : On Sunday 8 March, as reported, *an immense portion of that stupendous eminence the cliff bordering the sea, about a quarter of a mile west of Folkestone, suddenly gives way and is precipitated below with great violence.* The footpath from Sandgate to Folkestone is severed.

1827 According to W.Topley FRS (1875) a landslip affects an area of 500 yards to the east of Encombe House as far as the church.

1885 Encombe House, now owned by the Misses Reilly, is endangered. Numerous springs and treacherous ground are doing their work; the southern side of the house is subsiding; great cracks are appearing in walls; windows are assuming a diamond shape and the pretty paving fronting the house has opened considerably. Amid its sylvan glories, Encombe House is doomed.

1893 A major disaster hits two thirds of Sandgate. On Saturday 4 March around 7 pm, a series of shocks resembling those of an earthquake send people rushing from their collapsing homes into the streets. Next morning movement renews. No one is hurt, but 200 houses are damaged of which 70 are rendered uninhabitable. On 5 March without delay L.Drake Brockman, Clerk to Sandgate Board of Health, notifies the Assistant Secretary, Local Government Board Whitehall: *The face of the cliff for the greater part of a mile has subsided; the main road is cracked in many places, the pavement torn up, the seawall bowed out and gas and water mains are broken and the smaller streets have received serious damage…many people of the poorer classes are homeless – the Coastguard have had to leave their barracks which are in a dangerous almost ruinous condition.*

*Preamble to *Statute of Sewers,* 5 Henry VIII

1893 Chasms up to 9ft wide appear at Encombe. In a flurry of telegrams, the Clerk appeals for an Inspector to come down at once and, on 6 March, Whitehall signals Mr. Walton's arrival at 4.48pm at Sandgate Station to inspect and advise.

The Local Government Board Whitehall concurs with the views of Mr. Rienzi Walton that it is of the utmost importance that steps should be taken without delay to convey subsoil water from high land. In *Nature* (16 March 1893) J.F. Blake analyses the geological problems and concludes: *this area always has been and always will be liable to landslips. The lie of the beds which produces this liability cannot be altered by human agency, but [it] may be reduced to a minimum by a suitable system of land drainage, which shall prevent the access of so large a body of water to so dangerous an area...*At the same time Blake dismisses the local current theory that the blowing up of the wrecks of the *Benvenue* and *Calypso* (1891 and 1892) off Sandgate Esplanade could have provoked the Landslip. The question then arises in the House of Commons to which Mundella, for the Board of Trade, answers NO. The Military Hospital escapes damage due to the War Dept's previous underdraining of the site.

Overall damage is estimated at £100,000. For Public Works alone, finance is the overriding problem. The Sandgate Local Board has already exceeded its borrowing powers and Whitehall has no powers under the Acts to sanction a further loan. The Mayor of Folkestone refers to the Lord Mayor of London who launches a National Appeal to which, among so many, Queen Victoria gives £25. Self-help is also evident; fund-raising events are organised and a benefit is held at St. George's, Langham Place (London) at which the Rev. Russell Wakefield, Sandgate's inspiring Vicar and Chairman of the Local Board, contibutes with song.

On 17 May 1893, the Rev. Russell Wakefield as joint treasurer of the Sandgate Relief Fund rallies the unanimous support of the General Committee to allot part of the relief funds (total £8741 19s 9d) for the Land Drain Scheme and for relaying street drainage. It is a matter of each help all and all help each, whether landowners or tradesmen, affected or unaffected: *I hold this scheme to be the best calculated to relieve our dear little town from a burden so sore that it ought to awaken the sympathy of every feeling soul.*

In May 1893, under the auspices of the Sandgate Local Board, Mr. Baldwin Latham MICE, submits a land drain scheme extending 500 yards at the back of the hillside with five collection points and five outlets to the sea (points south of Littlebourne Lodge to Coastguard) in order to secure the recent landslip area from further subsidence and to protect the foundations of houses locally. By August, huts, men, wagons, horses and materials are on site. Within six months this land drain system, vital to Sandgate's stability and prosperity, is practically complete.

1895 The Sandgate Landslip Relief Fund holds its final meeting on 15 March. It reports that the system of land drainage designed and supervised by Mr. Balwin Latham continues to act efficiently and is satisfactory not only to the engineers, Henry Hill of Maidenhead, who carried out the works but to the Local Authority. For nearly seventy years Sandgate comes to enjoy relative stability.

STORM AND COAST EROSION: For centuries the sea has been encroaching on the Castle walls and is inexorably the main invasion threat to Sandgate, retreating only to strike again according to wind, tide and current. Clearly, the process of coast erosion gains momentum due in part to extensive works and groyning to the west of Sandgate (Redman 1852). In particular, the massive inundations of 1808 have forced Sir John Honeywood to build an embankment – three quarter million cubic yards of shingle – to protect the low-lying area between Seabrook and Hythe, fronting the Royal Military Canal. Hythe's gain leads to Sandgate's loss. An ongoing saga of damage and disaster follows. (Listed in Author's volume of evidence to Hythe Marina public inquiry 1987).

1844 In April, the Surveyor of Highways at Cheriton reports to the Inspector General of Fortifications:... *the sea has been encroaching for many years on this part of the coast and the late gales in conjunction with very high spring tides [have] caused several breaches in it.* Large portions of footpath have been carried away, causing public danger. Again in 1873, high tide and gale carries away many yards of road at Battery Point.

1876-7 Over New Year, a devastating gale causes extensive flooding in the Seabrook area endangering the Canal, and large quantities of stonework at Sandgate Castle are dragged away. In 1881 a new seawall and groynes extending as far as a low water mark, further impede the littoral drift to Sandgate. (William Muirhead & Partners Report 1933).

1880 Contractors are removing shingle at the only gap in the seawall between Hythe and Sandgate, denuding the natural defences. The Board of Trade Harbours Dept. requests the RNLI, who own the Boathouse foreshore, to prohibit or lease the right to remove shingle whether above or below ordinary high-water mark.

1894 In January a southerly gale ravages Sandgate and its sea defences. The Hythe and Sandgate Tramway Co. comes to a halt, the metals along the Esplanade being seriously undermined.

1889 The seawall at the west end of Sandgate Esplanade fronting Battery Point is almost destroyed; the sea has undermined the Lifeboat House; gas pipes are laid bare.

1900 Ford Madox Ford sums up the beleaguered village: *The sea, as a rule, is sleepy and washes the foot of the wall with a lazy murmur. But once a year – more often in some years – it wakes up and makes a plaything of the wall, tears great masses out of it, and carries them off to some unknown depths. This is particularly the case at the juncture of Seabrook and Sandgate [where] because of its situation in the bottom of the bay, the sea invariably works its winter will.*

1906 The Royal Commission on Coast Erosion (1906-11) takes evidence from Sandgate UDC. It finds that the whole of the Sandgate seaboard, about 1900 yards, is subject to beach starvation. Comparing maps of 1871 with 1898 at least half the foreshore shows an average 32ft. erosion. The principal conclusions point to the effects of the prevailing winds and impediments to the littoral drift which in Sandgate's case is west to east.

1929 A tidal wave, 10-12ft above ordinary sea-level, sweeps up the beach and within 10 minutes attains high-water mark, then collapses and vanishes as quickly as it came. It is thought to be a recurrence of some deep disturbance under the seabed, as in 1812.

1935 Folkestone is swept by the worst gale for many years; Sandgate flooded; blocks of concrete removed from Prince's Parade which the S.E. Railway Co. has long since left in disrepair.

1937 H.M.Office of Works, London, is aware of the threat to the sea defences and has admitted responsibility for upkeep of the groynes (letter 1932). Now they shift the onus onto frontagers who naturally contest this. The War years follow and deterioration is rapid.

1945 Owner of a Coastguard cottage, Max Ritson, reminds the Office of Works of pre-war negligence and signals a 10ft drop in beach levels, exposing the seawall to the full force of the prevailing SW winds: *The cottages shake as though near to an exploding bomb.* The Works Dept. routinely inspects. Nothing is done.

1949-51 Storms devastate the whole Sandgate seafront; the South bastion of the Castle is undermined; May Terrace collapses; Devonshire Terrace flooded; the Coastguard terrace is breached; the Seapoint Café and Bathing Establishment (formerly Taylor & Waddell c.1829) is totally destroyed; the waves bang out a mournful tune as a grand piano drifts to a watery grave. Matters are now desperate.

1952 The Sandgate and Western Folkestone Works Scheme goes into effect under the Coast Protection Act of 1949 and by means of the Acquisition of Land Act 1946. A new seawall extending from Sea Point on Sandgate Esplanade east to Radnor Cliff is built by Demolition and Construction Co. Ltd. Designed by Sir William Halcrow & Partners, consulting engineers, it has a concrete apron reinforced with steel sheet piling, but without bullnose to offset the waves. The Exchequer bears the cost, almost £200,000 by grant and 20-year loan. Certain frontagers are required to contribute.

1953 A North Sea surge assails the coastline with the highest tides in 20 years.

1962 The Minister of Housing and Local Government decides that Coast Protection shall become a national charge and that no more works schemes shall be made for the purpose of recovering compulsory contributions from private interests. However, it reminds Coast Protection Authorities of their powers to obtain contributions by agreement where substantial properties such as hotels, holiday camps stand to gain. This move by a Conservative Government relieves large landowners, such as the Radnor Estate, who border on the sea. In April 1985 Coast Protection passes to MAFF (Min. of Agric. Fisheries and Food).

1960-90 Storms are too many to recount in detail, among them 1967-76-81-83-87. Each is 'the worst gale in living memory' until the next leaves its trail. The sea defences fail; in certain areas the beach levels drop 20ft; sheet piling and footing of the new seawall is dangerously exposed. Overtopping and breaches in the seawall, deposits of shingle across the Trunk Road, flooding in the High Street and damage to shops and homes impose a heavy burden on Sandgate residents who cope as best they can. East Sandgate is often cut off from west Sandgate and through the efforts of Alex Todd of Encombe, a Public Footpath is established along the back of Sandgate from Wilberforce Road to Brewers Hill. Residents in high risk areas are offered sandbags as each winter approaches.

Above: *May Terrace undermined in storm December 1951. Now Martello Car Park.*
Below: *Ferocious storm, December 1981, smashes seawall under Devonshire Terrace, Author (foreground) temporarily homeless.* Folkestone Herald

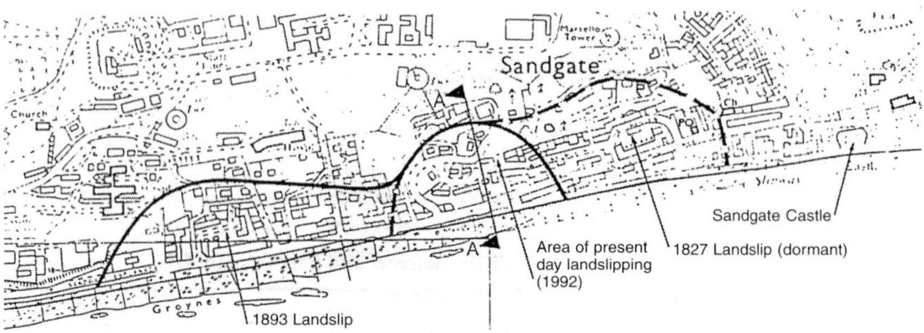

1958 **EARTH MOVEMENT REACTIVATED, 20thC:** The Kent Development Plan is confirmed. It zones the notorious Sandgate hillside for residential development heedless of liability to earth movement, flooding and subsidence. The Folkestone Borough Council, in an unprecedented act of land-greed and folly, has failed in its duty to comment.

In February 1958 the Folkestone and District Water Company overhaul the high-level Reservoir NW of Encombe heights which, since its installation after World War 1, is beset with problems. In November 1958 the cliff gives way behind Encombe. The Reservoir is abandoned, while new buildings and a swimming pool at the Camp show signs of cracking.

1962 Land & Property Development Co. Ltd. (a group of major Folkestone builders) obtains planning consent to develop the Encombe site on the basis of a limited Halcrow Report (April 1960) prepared for a previous owner for another purpose. Planning stipulations are ignored. Eight thousand tons of earth are shifted around; the contours of the land are entirely altered; fault lines are disregarded; fine and mature trees which have bonded the earth and absorbed water are hacked down despite Tree Preservation Orders. The whole pattern of natural and artificial land drainage is totally disrupted. The ornamental Water Gardens, designed to drain off surface and spring water, are utterly destroyed.* Most damaging, the 1893 Land Drain system which has provided a measure of stability for nearly 70 years is, undoubtedly, torn-up.

Sites are sold off. Unsuspecting newcomers move in. In future, the Council is obliged to draw attention to the terrain. Around 1970, 'Latchgate conditions' are imposed on new construction in parts of Sandgate but are no safeguard to adjacent properties.

1966 Predictably, destabilisation is widespread. Residents report tremors and both public and private property are affected. Between 1963 and 1980 Encombe House terrace subsides three times, a total of 10 ft. Settlement, fractured service pipes (80 recorded incidents between 1966-72), damaged houses, cracked roads are evident, and the seawall is at risk. Folkestone Borough Council turns its back on a serious situation: *Private property is not the Council's concern.* Local residents exert pressure, notably Alex Todd.

1967 Only the damning report on the Aberfan disaster stirs the Council into action. Halcrows undertake a preliminary survey. In October they admit that recent movements in Wilberforce Road and Sandgate High Street clearly indicate that parts of the ground are in a delicate state of equilibrium – also that earthworks carried out by the developers could have given rise to various disturbances *but this cannot be satisfactorily proved or disproved.*

*At one time the Sandgate Laundry drew off 100,000 gallons per week before burning down (c.1954).

1968 Halcrows recommend two test borings only, on the hillside. Drilling is underway when Coastguard resident telegraphs the Mayor of Folkestone, urgently requesting a *third test boring on public property as close to toe of slip as possible.* Subsequently, this takes place near the Sir John Moore statue. Kent River Authority is unable to consider a land drainage scheme.

1970 The Ministry of Housing and Local Government inspects and agrees to contribute to a Coast Protection Scheme to arrest or reduce the movement. Certain Councillors under a false impression (as can be proved) insist that residents, scattered across west Sandgate, must contribute or *nothing* will be done. The Ministry also adds: *Additionally [the Council] may wish to consider methods such as beach feeding to maintain the foreshore in the vicinity of the Encombe Estate (sic), 4-5ft above the tops of the piles in order to increase the factor of safety against the slip.* Halcrows, consistently maintain that the high cost of beach feeding (i.e. road transport) is out of proportion to the marginal benefit of additional stability it would provide (Aug 1977).

1972 Four houses on Sandgate High Street (Nos 156-162) are so badly cracked they have to be demolished. The site becomes Wilberforce Green. Ludlow's garages, some thirty on Hillside, are in ruins. The site becomes the Wilberforce Car Park.

1974 Shepway District Council, the new local authority, inherits an ugly situation on two fronts – earth movement to the north and coast erosion accompanied by loss of toe-weighting, to the south. In 1977, slippages occur in the Riviera area.

1978 Halcrows design a Well-point scheme on Encombe to intercept ground water flowing at deep level. Encombe House, now empty and derelict, burns down in mysterious circumstances (4 Oct).

1979 Shepway DC report: *The Encombe Drainage Scheme has recently been completed and this should reduce the flow of water running down the hill.*

1986 Halcrows state that the present movement started in the period 1931 and 1957 and, thereafter, the land-mass moved 4.0 metres seaward. They also admit that the Well-point scheme is proving ineffectual: *Much larger quantities of rainfall are entering the landslip than those intercepted by the well-points and a substantial inflow of water may be entering from other locations unknown.*

Meanwhile, severe storms in the 70's and 80's increase the rate of coast erosion; beach levels are at an all-time low; timber and ironwork groynes are beyond repair; large sections of vertical seawall and promenade as far as Hythe are breached or undermined; the Trunk Road is at risk. Halcrows now advise beach feeding (i.e. toe-weighting) as the cheapest of three stabilisation methods.

1988 A developer applies for Planning Permission to build three blocks of flats on the Encombe plateau. The planning officer who recommends acceptance, resigns a few weeks earlier to set up in Sandgate as an independent planning consultant, and to the developers. The Planning Committee reads a detailed report compiled by a knowledgeable local resident and holds a site meeting. Permission is refused. In 1990 a Public Inquiry is held on the subject of relevant conditions in the new Shepway District Local Plan. The Inspector turns down a specific objection: *There can however be no absolute guarantee [concerning] the period of time which will be needed to allow the upper land on which the Encombe site is located, to settle,* and the Council would have to be satisfied that development would not initiate any further instability.

1990 **COASTAL ENGINEERING AND BEACH MANAGEMENT:** Encombe Stabilisation Scheme (£2.5 million), a major undertaking starts in June. Harbour and General instal deep dowelling (164 dowels) along a 400 m. beach front, as a retaining force. The Ordnance Survey continues to monitor movement, heave and creep.

1991-2 The prevailing littoral drift is West to East. Shingle can only flow to Sandgate from the Hythe Ranges and this area is already impoverished. As part of the Encombe Scheme, beach replenishment is vital. Barges offload granite boulders from Norway to form four tapered groynes strategically placed between Granville Parade and Sandgate Esplanade. These are designed to retain a vast tonnage of offshore shingle pumped onto the beach to provide toe-weighting, to absorb wave energy and protect the exposed seawall. It is an amazing scene – not least when *Ajax* the pumping vessel is driven onto the reef south of the Coastguard terrace, in a fierce August gale.

1994-6 **HYTHE COAST PROTECTION STRATEGY** at long last halts the dangers of coast erosion (1.5 metres a year) between West Hythe and Sandgate where beach levels are lowest and the wave climate most severe. The extensive scheme designed by Posford Duvivier, eminent coastal engineers, costs £18.1 million, funded 75% by MAFF and the balance split between KCC and Shepway. These seaborne works along 5 Kms of coast resemble those off Encombe. In this case, the Twiss Road and Battery Point groynes come from a limestone quarry near Boulogne. Initially the shingle derives from Owers Bank off the Isle of Wight then, in 1996, from Hastings Bank (both licensed dredging sites) which saves time and money. Dredging vessels *Geopotes 14, Sand Heron* and *Sandpiper* are a friendly sight by day, and dazzling by night.

According to storm patterns the beach, as necessary, is regraded. Shattered sea defences, overtopping of the Trunk Road, inland flooding are no longer a recurrent nightmare. Can man out-engineer the forces of nature ? That is the long term test. Meanwhile the benefits justify the costs and SANDGATE AND ITS NEIGHBOURS GAIN A NEW LEASE OF LIFE.

Sandgate Esplanade. Mountainous seas lash seawall and Trunk Road

Right: *Dowel-piles or ground anchors are installed 23m deep on beach below Coastguard terrace, August 1990.*

Below: *Rock groynes will retain new supplies of pumped shingle*

1962 **CONSERVATION, A KEY ISSUE:** Developers have their eye on Sandgate's unique setting. Interesting old properties are bull-dozed; greed and collusion are getting their way. Sandgate's oldest surviving coaching inn, the Royal Kent Hotel (formerly 'The New Inn' c.1775) has been wilfully neglected with a view to cashing in on site value and, in view of an earlier outline planning permission (16 May 1961), the owner is entitled to demolish or be compensated. Tragically, the very heart of Sandgate is torn out, but not before Mrs Estelle Greenwall (Chairman) has founded The Sandgate Society (affiliated to the Civic Trust) for the future protection of an interesting village so pleasantly situated. From then on, it is an unremitting struggle.

1967 Fortunately, the enlightened Civic Amenities Act addresses the serious national loss of townscape heritage and it directs Local Authorities to designate 'areas of special architectural or historical interest, the character of which it is desirable to preserve and enhance' trees and open spaces included. Residents with local knowledge are encouraged to submit their views.

1969 Folkestone Borough Council is blind to Sandgate's merits and deaf to the pleas of The Sandgate Society. The proposed Conservation Area virtually ends where Sandgate begins, save for a tiny area around the Castle.

1970 As a last ditch effort, a longtime resident prepares a comprehensive written and photographic survey of the village. On behalf of The Sandgate Society, she submits this to the Kent County Planning Officer who perceives the case for Conservation.

1972 Finally, after inspection and many months of negotiation between County and Borough authorities and The Sandgate Society, inroads are halted. Two large areas, east and west, are designated for Conservation, and any changes are required to complement the present character. (Uglification does, in fact, creep in). This policy is reinforced in the Planning Policy Guidelines No. 15 *Planning and the Historic Environment* (Dept. of the Environment and Dept. of National Heritage, 1994) and incorporated in the Shepway 5-year District Plan.

1975 Shepway District Council, as required, publishes the *Sandgate Study, An Informal District Plan.* This is a wide appraisal of its socio-economic structure, of its landscape and townscape and also its traffic and parking problems. It also documents, with sketches, its streets and properties both listed and unlisted, with suggestions for future growth, enhancement and amenities. The survey is concerned for the trees which clothe the slopes and crests and help to bond the terrain. Already in 1973 six Tree Preservation Areas are carefully defined with the help of Sandgate Society members who identify and map the species. The survey also notes the lack of open space for recreational activity (save for four acres off Military Hill) and looks to the open area near Prince's Parade to offset the deficiency. In 1986, however, the loss of public open space is imminent.

1986 Southern Spas Ltd. (Hants) a company with no trading record, obtains 5-years exclusivity in partnership with Shepway DC to develop *Port Hythe* on 14 hectares of public land fronting and including Prince's Parade, in Shepway ownership. It will include and sever the Royal Military Canal and through road as far as the Hotel Imperial golf course. This environmentally dangerous and self-serving proposal, with outer harbour and lock-gate, entails 511 residential units including eleven blocks of seafront flats, 491 berths, 1,362 parking spaces (of which 80 for the public) and 45,000 sq ft. for commerce. In 1987, Southern Spas Ltd. enters into a one-share exchange with

J.S. Bloor Ltd. who take control, with Moore and Blatch of Southampton (W.J.R. Barrington of Dibden Purlieu) acting for them.

The Seabrook Association (Bernard Binns) and The Sandgate Society (Mrs L. René-Martin) lead the campaign to save this scenic and environmentally vulnerable coastline. Supporters include many amenity societies – ramblers, riders, sea and freshwater anglers and wildlife interests – also the Romney Marsh Research Trust and military historians concerned to preserve the historic Royal Military Canal, the Sluice Gate and remains of the Redoubt – all Scheduled Ancient Monuments linking with Sandgate's western defences.

1987 On 10 November, on the verge of a four-and-a-half week Public Inquiry at Shepway Civic Centre, the DoE on the revised recommendation of Lord Montagu of Beaulieu (Chairman of English Heritage) faxes Scheduled Monument Consent to truncate and distort 1400 m. of the Canal, abutting Sandgate. *Unfortunately,* writes Lord Montagu, *we have found no way of persuading the developers to avoid damage to the Canal altogether.* This pre-emptive move directly contravenes provisions of the Ancient Monuments and Archaeological Areas Act 1979. The Sandgate Society cannot afford Judicial Review. Geoffrey Edmunds, MA(Cantab) Hon FCIT, on behalf of the Sandgate community, spends nine months of unremitting time, toil and personal expense in seeking revocation of Consent and is met by endless Ministerial and bureaucratic evasions and manoeuvres. Finally, on 16 January 1990 Nicholas Ridley, Secretary of State for the Environment, is minded to approve the Planning Application subject to certain conditions.

1990 Following the grant of outline Planning Permission to Southern Spas Ltd., it falls upon Port Hythe Marina Developments (Kent) Ltd. and Shepway District Council to seek a Private Act of Parliament for the construction of harbour works, lock-gate and associated purposes. Bernard Binns for the Seabrook Association and Geoffrey Edmunds on behalf of the Sandgate community, petition against the Bill. A 30-clause Petition is deposited on the grounds that the proposed works will place the village of Sandgate and its residents at risk and will be injurious to their rights, property and interests. In July 1990, Geoffrey Edmunds assisted by Mrs L. René-Martin, attends 13 sessions of the House of Commons Select Committee over a 6-week period. The Seabrook Association is backed by Professor J.N. Hutchinson, C'Eng FICE and Jack Gill, MICE (Hydraulics). The promoters of the Bill have unlimited means to engage top lawyers, and eight expert witnesses. It is a David/Goliath battle. Finally, the Select Committee (two Conservative, two Labour) throw the Bill out, by three votes to one.

1991 The Royal Military Canal, one of the largest linear defensive works in the country is designated a Scheduled Ancient Monument in its entirety from Sandgate's border to Cliff End in Sussex.

1992 Among Sandgate's loveliest assets, the scenic footpaths across and around Shorncliffe Camp have been closed in order to guard the Garrison against possible terrorist attack. After several years of negotiation, Geoffrey Edmunds leads The Sandgate Society to victory at a Magistrate's hearing. The Ministry of Defence agrees to keep the perimeter paths open and in good condition, and a new Escarpment Path (from the Corniche to Military Hill) is made definitive. The Ministry enters into an unique legal undertaking to restore and reinstate all Rights of Way once the perceived threats are over, or, in the event the land over which they pass be sold or vacated.

1994 J.S. Bloor Ltd. drop their application for Scheduled Monument Consent for works to the Royal Military Canal, and allow outline planning permission for Port Hythe to lapse in 1995.

1997 The Ramblers Assn. gains a continuous footpath along this beautiful and historic Canal. The Shepway Policy Plan designates the Princes Parade area for recreation and tourism and directs that the majority of the site should remain open, and for a local park to service the needs of Seabrook.

1987 **NEW LOOK, NEW LIFE IN SANDGATE:** Sad to say, after ten years occupation the fast expanding SAGA Holiday Group leaves the lovely, half-wooded Enbrook Estate for the long empty Bouverie House in Folkestone, acquired for £1,250,000. Before doing so, SAGA obtains Outline Planning Permission to develop thc 27-acre site and for the conversion of Enbrook House, a Grade II Listed Building. Prior to departure, SAGA makes over to Shepway, for Sandgate's enjoyment, the strip of woodland alongside Military Road, – a delightful 'wild-life stroll' through which the Enbrook stream cascades down to the High Street.

Wimpey Homes Ltd. becomes the new owner and a confusing series of piecemeal applications and amendments follow. Despite local objections to scale and design, on 10 May 1989 Wimpeys are granted Detailed Planning Permission to saturate the prime site with over 300 small terraced properties and flats, subject to improved site access to the High St. In 1991, a Ministry of Transport Public Inquiry upholds the scheme with an estimated loss of 24 parking spaces, a serious blow to traders on the south side of the High Street. The Inspector, however, admits that Sandgate's parking situation is 'grotesque' and adds: *There can be very few comparable communities in the country whose High Street is a trunk road carrying 15,500 vehicles per day which have not long been bypassed at the expense of central funds.*

1995-7 The housing market is stagnant. SAGA Group buys back the estate from Wimpeys who are drawing in their horns. SAGA decides to concentrate their forces in the SAGA Building in Folkestone and in Sandgate; public consultations follow, and Listed Building Consent permits the demolition of Enbrook House. An ultra-modern complex arises, similar to the Inland Revenue HQ at Nottingham, designed by Michael Hopkins and Partners. Initially, the glass-cladded offices will hold 800 staff with an imposing, tent-like Amenity Centre alongside. Known as the 'Saga Pavilion' it will include a restaurant, child care facilities and will host a multitude of activities such as concerts and performances by local Arts Groups. There will be public access to the beautiful, partly-wooded grounds. Roger de Haan, Saga Chairman with a seeing eye and a listening ear, becomes Vice-President of The Sandgate Society.

1998 SAGA aim to restore an ornamental lake with aquatic plants, as part of the 'wild-life stroll' along the Enbrook stream. Land they have made over to Shepway, just west of St. Paul's will provide eight public parking spaces to compensate in part for the loss of others; the familiar rag-stone wall around Enbrook Park is reinstated; traffic flow problems in central Sandgate are under review. A wind of change is blowing through the area, and the community at large is proud to have SAGA Group, a prestigious and caring enterprise in their midst once again.

In Conclusion

SANDGATE'S rise and progress is unending. Volumes of fascinating and still unpublished history reside in one small village and its environs. What it was, what it is and can become depends on each new generation. So far, the work of the 'village elders' and, since 1962, the unremitting efforts of Sandgate Society members and others, have succeeded in preserving much of its enchantment where land meets sea.

Progress, inevitably, puts pressure on landscape and townscape. Those who love to live in Sandgate, or visit, are often saddened at unwelcome inroads. They are concerned at the thinning and neglect of the lovely wooded slopes, haven of birds and wildlife, with glimpses through the foliage of an everchanging sea. They regret the loss of High Street trade to distant supermarkets. They see blocks of flats obtruding where one house stood before. Above all, they deplore the noisy A 259 Trunk Road which engulfs the narrow High Street and urgently needs to be diverted.

But progress can be positive. When all seems nearly lost, changes come about. For the time being, the coastline is protected from further erosion and sea flooding. Inland, storm water control is a SWA priority. Prince's Parade and the Royal Military Canal are preserved for public enjoyment and local footpaths too. Entirely through local initiative, the Chichester Memorial Hall and the old Volunteer Fire Station are saved for community use. The essential Public Library is restored. The designation of two large Conservation Areas (1972) confers some degree of protection, and caring residents and dealers have sensitively restored their properties. While, looking to the future, Sandgate is conscious that preservation and enhancement can, within strict bounds, go hand in hand with careful, innovative development which benefits the community.

Sandgate's roots and continuity are precious. If it is to survive as Cobbett sees it – 'a beautiful little place upon the beach itself' then vigilance is needed. More than ever, it is vital that all should aid and cherish it, especially the young. If this brief history encourages them to do so then the endeavours of previous generations will not have been in vain.

LINDA RENÉ-MARTIN

ACKNOWLEDGMENTS: This work draws on many sources: Public Records Office, Kew; British Library MSS Dept; Lambeth Palace Archives; National Maritime Museum, Greenwich; Ville de Calais Archives; Shepway DC Engineers; KCC Heritage Room in Folkestone Public Library, particularly the extensive Fynmore Scrapbooks; RIBA Library; New York Public Library; Beinecke Library (Yale); The Royal Star & Garter Home, Richmond; Sandgate Society Archives; H. Margary, Lympne Castle; and William Drummond, London. Diagram (p.40) by permission ICE, London: Slope Stability Engineering 1991, M.J. Palmer M.Sc. F.G.S. To all, my thanks are due. Also for useful sidelights from local residents including Margaret Todd, Patricia Wren, Ann Nevill and Fred Moore.

My special thanks go to Anne Roberts for her technical expertise and patience in preparing the text for press.

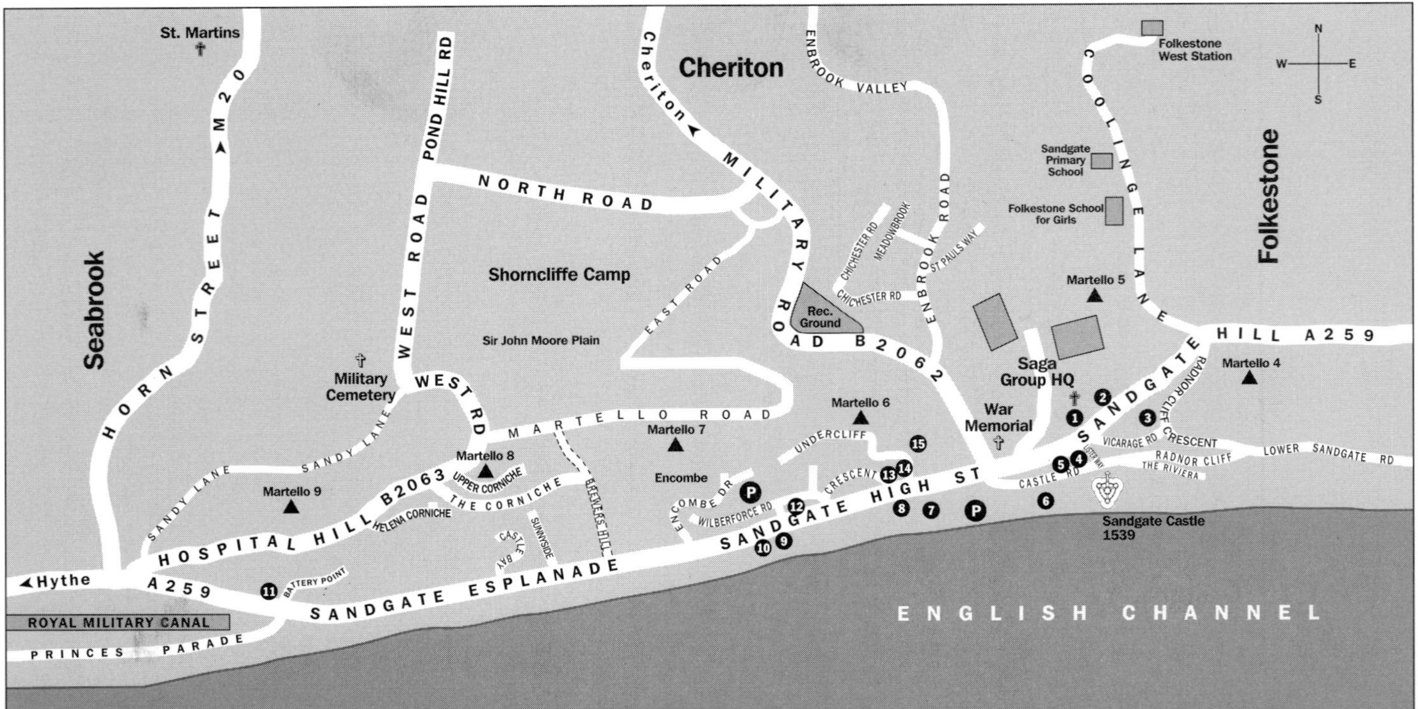

SIMPLIFIED MAP OF SANDGATE, EXTENT 2½ KMS approx. Main thoroughfares only; the many side roads, lanes and footpaths not shown

1. Church of St Paul (1850)
2. Shipwrights Cottages (c.1773)
3. Spade House, H.G. Wells (1901-1910)
4. Former National School (1866)
5. KCC Public Library
6. T/S Invicta, Sea Cadets, Castle Rd
7. Folkestone Rowing Club, Granville Parade
8. Old Fire Station (1884) Sandgate Soc. HQ
9. Old Coastguard Station (1896)
10. Sir John Moore Statue, Esplanade
11. Battery Point c.1800 Scheduled Ancient Monument
12. Little Theatre (FHODS)
13. Post Office
14. Chichester Hall (1913)
15. 2nd Sandgate Scouts Centre, Undercliff